SPAIN

on

BACKROADS

DUNCAN PETERSEN

HUNTER
PUBLISHING INC

300 Raritan Center Parkway,
CN 94, Edison, N.J. 08818

SPAIN
On
BACKROADS

The Motorist's Guide to the Spanish Countryside

DUNCAN PETERSEN

HUNTER
PUBLISHING INC

300 Raritan Center Parkway,
CN 94, Edison, N.J. 08818

First published in the UK and Commonwealth
1994 by
Duncan Petersen Publishing Ltd,
54, Milson Road,
London, W14 0LB

ISBN 1 872576 39 7

First published in the USA 1994 by
Hunter Publishing Inc.,
300 Raritan Center Parkway,
Edison, NJ 08818
Tel (908) 225 1900 Fax (908) 417 0482

ISBN 1-55650-637-6

Conceived, edited and designed by
Duncan Petersen Publishing Ltd,
54, Milson Road,
London, W14 0LB

Sales representation in the UK and Ireland by
World Leisure Marketing,
117, The Hollow, Littleover, Derby, DE3 7BS
Tel 0332 272 020 Fax 0332 774 287
Distributed by
Grantham Book Services

Typeset by Duncan Petersen Publishing Ltd
Originated in Italy by Reprocolor International, Milan
Printed in Italy by G. Canale & C. SpA, Turin

A CIP catalogue record for this book is available from
the British Library

Editorial director Andrew Duncan
Assistant editor Nicola Davies
Art director Mel Petersen
Design assistants Chris Foley, Beverley Stewart

Picture credits
Numerals refer to the tour numbers given in Contents, page 9: 1, 2,3 **Adam Hopkins** *(also
pages: 1 and 10)*; 4,5,6 **John Lloyd** *(also page 5)*; 7 **James Scrubie**; 8, 9 **Fiona Duncan and
Caroline Sharpe**; 10 **Adam Hopkins**; 11,12,13 **John Lloyd**; 14 **Nick Inman & Clara Villanueva**
(also page 3); 15 Adam Hopkins; 16, 17, 18, 19, 20 **Nick Inman & Clara Villanueva**.

• Information on opening and closing times, and telephone numbers, was correct at time of publication, but those who run hotels, restaurants and tourist attractions are sometimes obliged to change times at short notice. If your enjoyment of a day out is going to depend on seeing, or eating at a certain place, it makes sense to check beforehand that you will gain admission.

• Many of the roads used for tours in this book are by-ways in the true sense: they have zero visibility at corners, they are too narrow for oncoming cars to pass, and they include hairpin bends and precarious mountain roads with sheer drops. Please drive with due care and attention, and at suitable speeds.

• Many of the roads used for tours in this book are in upland areas. During winter, they could be closed by snow. Consult a motoring organization or local tourist office if in doubt.

Every kilometre of *Spain on Backroads* was not only planned and written, but personally driven by a team of Hispanophile writers and local experts:

The tours covering **Galicia**, the **Picos de Europa, Rioja, Ciudad Rodrigo** and **Extremadura** are by Adam Hopkins. He first visited Spain as a schoolboy and has never looked back: his first two jobs were in Spain; he has written about Spain and Spanish affairs over the years in British newspapers and he keeps regular contact with Spanish friends and places. He is the author of *Spanish Journeys: a Portrait of Spain* published by Penguin (1993) and, with Gabrielle Macphedran, of an illustrated guide to Spain.

The Western Pyrenees, Central Pyrenees, Costa Brava and the **Garrotxa**, the **Maestrazgo**, the **Serrania de Cuenca** and **Teruel** and the **Sierra de Albarracin** are the work of John Lloyd. Formerly the editor of a leisure magazine, he has been a freelance writer for several years, contributing to newspapers, magazines and books. He has travelled widely in Spain, by road, rail and on foot, and feels most at home in the country's under-rated wilder inland areas.

Nick Inman and Clara Villanueva devised **Inland from the Costa Blanca, Sierra de Cazorla, La Campina,** the **White Towns**, the **Alpujarras** and **The Almerian Desert**. They have been exploring and writing about off-beat and out-of-the-way Spain for the past five years. They write regularly for *Lookout*, Spain's English-language magazine; they are authors of *Excursions in Eastern Spain* and together edit the annual *Charming Small Hotel Guide to Spain.*

Cuidad Rodrigo is the work of James Scrubie, who has made Madrid his home for several years; **Sierra de Gredos** is by Caroline Sharpe, freelance travel writer; and **Sierra de Guaderrama** by Fiona Duncan, travel author and editor, who has travelled extensively in the Madrid area. She is co-author of several of the *American Express Pocket Travel Guides* and of *Spain The Versatile Guide*, to be published in 1995.

Contents

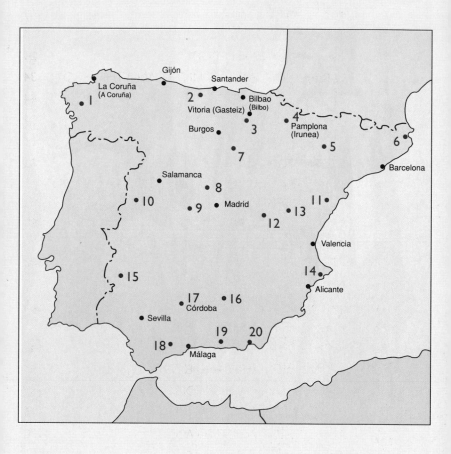

Gijón

La Coruña
(A Coruña)

1

Santander

2

Bilbao
(Bilbo)

Vitoria (Gasteiz)

4

Pamplona
(Irunea)

Burgos

3

5

6

Barcelona

7

Salamanca

8

9

Madrid

10

13

11

12

Valencia

14

15

Alicante

17

16

Córdoba

Sevilla

19

20

18

Málaga

The tours are arranged in a north-south sequence, beginning in Galicia in north-western Spain, and ending in the south, with Andalucia.

• *In the Picos.*

This guide is the fourth in a series devoted to driving country roads. It was easy to introduce the predecessors, covering France, Britain and Italy, with a neat summary of the delights of driving the backroads of those countries. Not so Spain.

Exploring rural Spain is an experience of a different kind. It can certainly be an adventure. You will, with this guide, visit places where strangers are rare enough to merit stares. Some of the landscapes you will drive through can only be described, in European terms, as extraordinarily varied: all within 100 kilometres, for example, you will find the Almerian Desert; the snow-capped Sierra Nevada; and Mediterranean coast of Granada.

Not only the geography, but the people are different, especially the country people, who can be exceptionally generous: generous enough to share their lunch with strangers or to provide the visitor with goods on the understanding that 'You'll pay tomorrow'.

The *Backroads* driving guides are for people who want to break free from the beaten track and get an extra dimension from travel. We have no hesitation in asserting that *Spain on Backroads* will do this for you, and more.

The routes   The 20 locations from the Pyrenees to Gibraltar have been chosen to give a taste of Spain's strikingly diverse countryside and little-recognized historic towns. Mostly figures-of-eight, except where geography requires something different, the tours can be driven in one or two days. But you will get more pleasure if you drive them in two or more – there is so much to enjoy that it would be a shame to treat them as rally driving courses.

Even taking them slowly, you will not have to stop at every attraction. Look on the routes as guides to help you find what interests you, not as military orders to be carried out to the letter. There are no prizes if you complete them in a given time – take them at the pace you enjoy and modify them to suit yourself.

Sometimes, however, time may be short. With an average length of around 170 km, the tours can be driven inside a day; do this and you will not be able to make many stops, but you will get the overall feeling of an area.

The itineraries have been carefully chosen to give a rounded mixture of pleasures: interesting backroads; beautiful countryside; arresting towns and villages; strong local identities; and, just occasionally, an unmissable major tourist attraction.

The roads   This book is about country roads; in Spain you must expect the worst. Many of the tours explore upland areas where roads wind tortuously through the hills. Others chart courses through country where motorists are few. Signposting, too, can be a nightmare; directions in the book are as exhaustive as possible, but a degree of patience will help you enjoy yourself more in the long run.

Signos convencionales
Explicação dos Signos

Zeichenerklärung
Legend · Légende

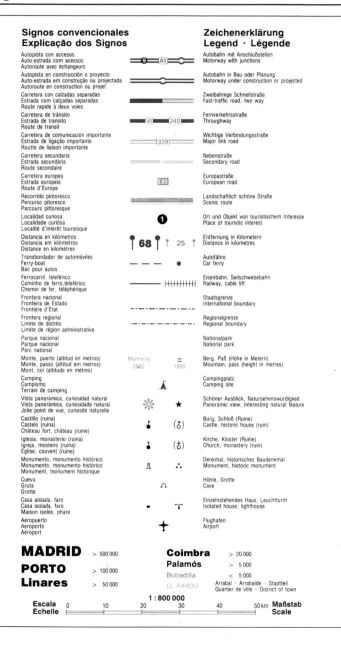

Autopista con accesos Auto-estrada com acessos Autoroute avec échangeurs	Autobahn mit Anschlußstellen Motorway with junctions
Autopista en construcción o proyecto Auto-estrada em construção ou projectada Autoroute en construction ou projet	Autobahn in Bau oder Planung Motorway under construction or projected
Carretera con calzadas separadas Estrada com calçadas separadas Route rapide à deux voies	Zweibahnige Schnellstraße Fast-traffic road, two way
Carretera de tránsito Estrada de transito Route de transit	Fernverkehrsstraße Throughway
Carretera de comunicación importante Estrada de ligação importante Routte de liaison importante	Wichtige Verbindungsstraße Major link road
Carretera secundaria Estrada secundária Route secondaire	Nebenstraße Secondary road
Carretera europea Estrada europeia Route d'Europe	Europastraße European road
Recorrido pintoresco Percurso pitoresco Parcours pittoresque	Landschaftlich schöne Straße Scenic route
Localidad curiosa Localidade curiósa Localité d'interèt touristique	Ort und Objekt von touristischem Interesse Place of touristic interest
Distancia en kilómetros Distancia em kilómetros Distance en kilomètres	Entfernung in Kilometern Distance in kilometres
Transbordador de automóviles Ferry-boat Bac pour autos	Autofähre Car ferry
Ferrocarril, teleférico Caminho de ferro,teleférico Chemin de fer, téléphérique	Eisenbahn, Seilschwebebahn Railway, cable lift
Frontera nacional Fronteira de Estado Frontière d'Etat	Staatsgrenze International boundary
Frontera regional Limite de distrito Limite de région administrative	Regionalgrenze Regional boundary
Parque nacional Parque nacional Parc national	Nationalpark National park
Monte, puerto (altitud en metros) Monte, passo (altitud em metros) Mont, col (altitude en mètres)	Berg, Paß (Höhe in Metern) Mountain, pass (height in metres)
Camping Campismo Terrain de camping	Campingplatz Camping site
Vista panorámica, curiosidad natural Vista panorâmica, curiosidade natural Jolie point de vue, curiosité naturelle	Schöner Ausblick, Natursehenswürdigkeit Panoramic view, interesting natural feature
Castillo (ruina) Castelo (ruina) Château fort, château (ruine)	Burg, Schloß (Ruine) Castle, historic house (ruin)
Iglesia, monasterio (ruina) Igreja, mosteiro (ruina) Eglise, couvent (ruine)	Kirche, Kloster (Ruine) Church, monastery (ruin)
Monumento, monumento histórico Monumento, monumento histórico Monument, monument historique	Denkmal, historisches Baudenkmal Monument, historic monument
Cueva Gruta Grotte	Höhle, Grotte Cave
Casa aislada, faro Casa isolada, faro Maison isolée, phare	Einzelnstehendes Haus, Leuchtturm Isolated house, lighthouse
Aeropuerto Aeroporto Aéroport	Flughafen Airport

MADRID > 500 000
PORTO > 100 000
Linares > 50 000

Coimbra > 20 000
Palamós > 5 000
Bobadilla < 5 000
EL PARDO Arrabal · Arrabalde · Stadtteil
Quartier de ville · District of town

1 : 800 000

Escala / Echelle 0   10   20   30   40   50 km Maßstab / Scale

The maps The routes are drawn on the general-purpose motoring maps at a scale of 1:800,000 produced by Ravenstein Verlag GmbH, Bad Soden / Ts..

The maps carry plenty of helpful information for the tourist and road user. However, in common with all mapping at this scale, not every single minor road is featured – some of the tours, indeed, use stretches of unmarked road – and the names of a few small settlements are omitted.

Spain has four official languages: Castellano, officially known as Spanish; Catalán, spoken in Cataluñya and Vallencia; Gallego (spoken in Galicia) and Euskera, spoken in the Basque country. With important place names the maps give both the local version and the Spanish (Castilian) version.

Hints on map-reading When on the road, map-read actively, rather than passively. This comes down to knowing where you are on the map all the time. It is essential to understand the implications of scale. On 1:800,000 mapping, one centimetre on the map represents 8 km on the ground. So for every kilometre you travel, you need to tick off mentally the appropriate portion of map. To do this, you need a point of reference from which to start – obvious landmarks present themselves continuously in the shape of villages and road junctions.

The route directions Printed in italics, throughout the text these are an aid to trouble-free navigation, not join-up-the-dots instructions for getting round the routes. They are most detailed on tricky stretches, especially when signposting is absent or when you have to follow roads not marked on the map. In a country that welcomes strangers, do not be afraid to ask directions if you get lost; even if your Spanish is not up to much, vigorous miming with a gracious smile will get you a long way.

Food   There is no denying that in some parts of Spain covered by the routes in this guide, restaurants are few. Best pack a picnic. Elsewhere, you may be pleasantly surprised at the pride taken in producing regional dishes and wine.

The Mediterranean food of Spain, featuring fresh fish, a splendid variety of vegetables, salad stuffs and fruit, compares with that of France.

Although the restaurant information was accurate at the time of going to press, remember that opening hours can change. While some establishments close on national holidays, it is by no means the rule. In some places, where visitors are rare out of season, restaurants and hotels often close in the quieter months. Where reliable information was available, the text points these out. Where no closing time is given it is reasonably safe to assume that the hotel or restaurant is open continuously. But sometimes hotels and restaurants close at the owners' discretion, or indeed their whim. You are advised to check in advance.

Hotels   Like the restaurant recommendations, these are not exhaustive. They are a selection of sound-value places, mostly on the routes, sometimes a short detour away from the marked route.

Fuel   In some parts of Spain, particularly rural backwaters, petrol stations are scarce. Major cities apart, they also close for a long lunchbreak – often from 12 to 4pm – and on Sundays. Fill up when possible in the morning.

National holidays   New Year's Day; Jan 6, Day of the Three Kings; Easter Monday; May 1, Labour Day; August 15, Assumption; Oct 12, first voyage to America; Nov 1, All Saints; Dec 8, Immaculate Conception; Christmas Day.

Opening hours   Shops generally open from 9.30 to 1.30 and from 4 to 8. Most close Saturday afternoon and Sunday, though in resorts during summer seven-day opening is common. Major department stores may be open over lunch.

Museums and other tourist attractions have widely varying opening times and it is best to check locally when details are not provided in the text.

THE PRICE BANDS

To give an indication of cost, three restaurant price bands are used. They represent approximate prices for a three-course lunch without wine.

Price band A   under 2,000 pesetas

Price band B   2,000-4,500 pesetas

Price band C   over 4,500 pesetas

Hotel price bands, representing the cost of a double room in mid-season, with breakfast, are:

Price band A   under 6,500 pesetas

Price band B   6,500-9,500 pesetas

Price band C   over 9,500 pesetas

Prices quoted were correct at the time of going to press, but, of course, are liable to increase. In most cases, however, increases will remain in proportion so that the price banding system is likely to remain useful.

Capital letters are not accented in this guide.

• *Walled harbour, Muros.*

There is more to the coastline of Galicia than you can get round in a week. This drive, rather longer than our usual, makes a rough circle of a small section of it, and will take two days at least, longer in swimming weather. It starts and ends at Santiago de Compostela, a useful centre with an airport and car hire facilities.

The coastline is deeply indented, pierced by long *rías* or estuaries, of great beauty but suprisingly kilometre-heavy. The route therefore concentrates on what we believe to be the highlights: the wilder upper reaches of the Rías Bajas; Cape Finisterre; and the fishing villages of the Costa de la Muerte. The Rías Bajas or Lower Estuaries lie on the west coast, rich in shellfish, well populated and often cultivated to the water's edge. But they turn wild and challenging as they approach the World's End, Cape Finisterre (in Galician, Fisterra). The Costa de la Muerte – Coast of Death – is one of the most impressive, gauntest, stretches of coast you can travel.

As a contrast to the seascapes, your route will be backed by a green interior, with field and forest, granite wayside crosses and long grey granite granaries, called *hórreos*.

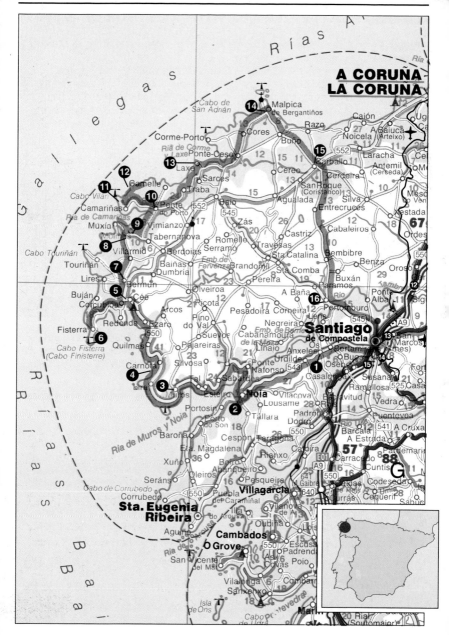

ROUTE: 290 KM, WITH A DETOUR OF 40 KM

Santiago de Compostela

Santiago, supposedly the burial-place of the Apostle St James and goal of pilgrims through the ages, is one of those satisfying cities where nothing jars and all falls into place – in this case as a moving exposition of Christian faith. Its very heart is the Portico de la Gloria, carved by the Romanesque Master Mateo to welcome pilgrims to the cathedral. The cathedral is cloaked in the great twin-towered Baroque façade known as the Obradoiro. Endlessly rewarding to wander among, churches, monasteries and university buildings abound, all built in local granite, as are the arcaded shopping streets. Umbrellas are pretty common, too: Santiago has plenty of rain. Buskers vie with students to give the city a youthful atmosphere.

Naturally, given pilgrims, there are hotels; and, given shellfish in the *rías* and excellent local produce from an agriculture helped along by wet weather, there are some outstanding restaurants. Galician wine comes sharp and young and sometimes slightly fizzy, and is often drunk from little china cups. (Note: restaurant prices vary sharply, rising sky-high if you go for delicacies such as lobster or *percebes* – goose barnacles. Otherwise, prices may be a little cheaper than some other parts of Spain.)

The best access-point to the historic city, with an underground car park, is the Plaza Galicia.

Los Reyes Catolicos
(hotel, Santiago de Compostela)

The Santiago parador, in the cathedral square, occupies the magnificent pilgrims' hospital endowed by Ferdinand and Isabel. It's a splendid place to stay. *Plaza del Obradoiro 1 (Plaza de Espaná 1); tel 981 582200; price band C.*

Middle-range hotels are also fairly numerous in Santiago and at the lower end of the scale there are small pensions, sometimes in apartments. Try, as I have often done, Mapoula, clean, central and economic at Entremurallas 10, *tel 981 580124; price band B/C.*

Vilas, Fornos and Casa Manolo
(restaurants, Santiago de Compostela)

The Restaurante Vilas, presided over by Josefina of the same name, is an authentically old-fashioned and thoroughly dignified Santiago shellfish restaurant. *Rosalía de Castro 88, tel 981 59 10 00/59 21 70; closed Sun; price band C.*

Fornos goes for the same type of food, more moderately priced, *Avenida General Franco 24; tel 981 56 57 21; closed Sun evening; price band B/C.*

Amazingly good-value dinners, and very hearty too, are served at Casa Manolo, *Rua Travesia 27; tel 981 58 29 50; closed Sun evening; price band A.*

From Santiago, set out south from the Plaza Galicia down the Rua da Senra as for Pontevedra, but shortly after Restaurante Vilas in C/ Rosalía de

• *The cemetery of Santa María Nuova, Noia.*

Castro, angle right for Noia down a road in due course revealed as C543.

Rosalía
(hotel, Los Angeles)

About 12 km from Santiago, turn left ① at village of Los Angeles (Galician: Os Anxeles). Continue 500 m for this 19thC stone house charmingly converted into a hotel. It has a restaurant; price band B.

After Los Angeles the (good) road becomes truly rural, with wood smoke rising from grey stone villages, and green of pine and eucalyptus. Haymakers here use pitchforks and may build their haystacks quite casually around a single upright pole.

Noia

About 30 km from Santiago, take the turn left for Noia Este, in fact descending 3.5 km to the centre of this attractive town ② at the head of its own ría – though, curiously, it seems to turn its back on the water. There is a fine alameda, a walkway with trees (sometimes, but not in Noia, grafted together overhead to make a single canopy) and an old town with dark and narrow streets. Here, there rises the Church of San Martín, with splendidly sculptural, weed-grown western façade. Back in the town itself, Sta María Nuova has strangely carved headstones, from the 9th to 19thC, showing the professions of the deceased.

Leaving Noia, you start to get the views that make the Rías Bajas so compulsive: enclosed tidal waters, with a sea entrance far away to the west, the far bank always in view from the one that you are driving,

19 ∎

• *Hórreo, Carnota.*

forested hills above with field and vineyard patchily set out along the water's edge. Here perhaps is a sawmill with a wooden hulk lodged in the tidal mud in front of it and there a beach of crystalline golden sand.

Muros Keeping always reasonably close to the water, with beaches beginning to occur more and more regularly, you come, about 36 km from Noia, to the old and settled fishing port ③ of Muros, where the arcades of the buildings behind the front are now sunk metres deep with time, and tiny alleys, only big enough for a fisherman, his oars and nets, lead up between the houses. There is a walled harbour; above, there is a pretty Romanesque church with an *hórreo* in front of it.

Casa Santolo Facing you at the northern end of the *alameda*, Casa Santolo is the
(restaurant, place the travelling salesmen eat at. Good fish and shell-fish, naturally.
Muros) *Calvario s/n; tel 981 82 01 96/82 29 06; closed Mon; price band A/B.*

A' Esmorga Leaving town, to the west beyond the harbour, A' Esmorga is on your
(restaurant, right, after about 200 m, up a concrete ramp. Bar meals downstairs: the
Muros) *vieira* or scallop comes in a rich brown sauce, a world away from effete

Coquilles Saint Jacques. Upstairs there is a smart dining room with fine *ría* views. *Paseo Bombe; tel 981 82 65 28; price band A/B.*

Soon after Muros, the road begins to turn the corner north out of the Ría de Muros (which becomes the Ría de Noia as it winds further inland), crossing a promontory. Soon, over more open seas, you will make out Cabo Fisterra to the north descending towards the water in the shape of a sugar mouse. The coast beside the road is now a composition of wild white beaches and lagoon. Suddenly the hills are mostly rock and scrub and then, as you come round the final corner into the village of Liria, you are in full *hórreo* country. The longest in all Galicia is here in the village (turn up right opposite the Alba insurance agency).

Carnota

About 20 km from Muros, is ④ the momentous beach of Carnota, a huge hoop of often almost empty sand, backed by marsh and agricultural land and mountains. It is exposed and shadeless, but those who appreciate this kind of landscape consider it possibly the finest beach in all Galicia. There are three main ways down to it: opposite the petrol station in Maceiros, first outpost of Carnota village; as signposted from the centre of Carnota; and finally where a river crosses the beach, just at its northern end. This is a popular spot, though liable to currents, so do be specially careful here.

Fisterra

The coast road, the only option, now winds north, passing above tempting coves, Cabo Fisterra continually growing larger. Passing through the industrial town of Cee (about 24 km on from Carnota), ⑤ turn left through older and more attractive Corcubión, with an *alameda* and glassed-in balconies. Now you get the delightful stretch of road that leads out on to Cabo Fisterra, winding through high pines and eucalyptus, almost by-passing the litte town of Fisterra and so to ⑥ the lighthouse on the cape (some 26 km from Cee).

It seems quite probable that early, pre-Christian pilgrimages through Santiago ended here at the westernmost point of the known world, and the cape itself is high and awesome, especially in rough weather with fishing boats working their way home around its rocks. The best views are at the top of a turning upwards, just before the (disappointing) lighthouse and passing the municipal rubbish tip with stinking bonfire (1 km, signposted Monte de Facho).

Fisterra itself is a quiet and unremarkable little fishing port, busy with visitors in summer. People drive out to Fisterra, spend a single night, eat a great fish dinner in one of several good restaurants and then head inland or along the coast.

Cabo Fisterra

(hotel/ restaurant, Fisterra)

This is the leading hotel in Fisterra (the Hostal Fisterra is a sister establishment), offering adequate accommodation and magnificent seafood – all, says proprietor Manolo Sanchez Iglesias, fished locally.

This is definitely not the case in Santiago. Photographs show Manolo with the Nobel Prize-winning writer Camilo José Cela, a Galician who knows a good thing when he eats it. *Santa Catalina s/n; tel 981 74 00 00; price band hotel A/B, restaurant B, though too much lobster could push it up to C.*

Muxía

Retracing your route via Corcubión, turn north along the C552. After three km, ⑦ take the left turn (CP2303) for Muxía, a further 16 km. This is a soothing inland drive, through low hills with woods, *hórreos* and cabbages, which are definitely big in Galicia. *⑧ At Albugueria, take short-cut left for Muxía and so to a first glimpse of the Ría de Camariñas. From this point, effectively, you are on the Costa de la Muerte.*

Muxía's mandatory sight is at the promontory's end, less than one km beyond the fishing harbour. Here on the wild sea's edge is a group of sacred rocks, one shaped somewhat like a pelvis, another a rocking stone which groans when it is moved by wind or bouncing crowds (as happens in the remarkable September fiestas). These rocks are associated with pre-Christian healing rituals, still surviving in somewhat dilute form. Pilgrims come from afar in hope of a cure or a guarantee of health or in fulfilment of a vow. Crawl upwards under the pelvic rock three times and you will never, ever have a kidney problem.

From Muxía, retrace, making for ⑨ the village of Molinos (Galician, Muiños). Just before the Renault garage (sign invisible until you have turned) take the minor road for Puente del Puerto. This is a particularly lovely drive along the ría's edge.

O'Atrevido
*(bar/
restaurant
with rooms
Puente del
Puerto)*

The Bar O'Atrevido, just left after the bridge in Puente, looks less than kempt but serves delicious food in home-made style. Carmen Novais (known locally as Chista), and her husband Manuel Canosa preside, with kindness and charm. There are very simple rooms upstairs. Improbably enough, English is spoken here. *C/ Outeiro, 51/53; tel 981 73 00 71; price band A.*

**Camariñas
and the
English
Cemetery**
(detour)

⑩ Continuing past the O'Atrevido to the west, the road leads to Camariñas and the so-called Cementerio de los Ingleses, the English cemetery, a there-and-back diversion of 40 km, highly recommended in fine weather. For reasons of safety, avoid the final stretch, whether on foot or in a car, in heavy weather.

Camariñas is, of course, a fishing harbour and beyond it (signs for Cabo Vilán or Villano) the road leads past a major electricity-generating wind park. The huge windmills look rather grim from Muxía, but even so they are impressive when you reach them, as is the exposed position of ⑪ the Cabo Villano lighthouse. *Just past the road into the windmills, take the dirt road to the right and follow the coastline north.* You cross one rocky ridge on a poor but passable surface and descend to a coastal terrain of beach and rock, inspirational or terrifying depending on the elements. *In due course another dirt road comes in from the right. Continuing about another km, down and to left, is* ⑫ the simple cemetery containing the remains of some 200 officers and cadets who shipped on the English training brig *Serpent* in 1890 and whose journey ended here in shipwreck and death. There were only three survivors. Nor is this by any means unique. Almost every year, lives are lost from almost every fishing harbour on the Costa de la Muerte.

Laxe   *Returning via Camariñas to Puente del Puerto, keep to the north side of the river, on the Vimianzo road. About 4 km later,* ⑬ *turn left for Laxe another fishing port (about 14 km). On reaching the coast (for a second time) at Laxe, hold left for the village, centred round an old church over the harbour.* Laxe, though north-facing and slightly ugly on the periphery, has a particularly fine beach.

Malpica   ⑭ *Malpica, the last of the fishing harbours on this circuit, lies some 25 km on, via Ponteceso (here avoiding the left turn for Cormes).* Though Malpica has scarcely a building of distinction, it is a great little town, with an inner and outer fishing harbour, both bustling, redolent of fish and fishing nets, mixed with a heady scent of paint and varnish. Anyone may stroll into the wholesale fishmarket, where men sell, women buy, on behalf of fish-factories and restaurants. The inshore fishermen set off at 9 pm. in a picturesque scene, with their food-baskets and lanterns, and often fish opposite the little town's excellent beach.

Hostal JB   There are several rather home spun fish restaurants above and around
(hostal,   the inner harbour. The Hostal JB makes a clean and friendly stopping
Malpica)   place – *on the Plaia Maior (or Main Beach); tel 981 72 09 62/72 19 06; price band A/B.*

After Malpica, it is relatively straightforward cross-country driving to Santiago, south-east via Carballo (19 km) and then almost due south. In Carballo, poorly signposted as we went to press, turn right just after the petrol station, which is on a left-hand bend, then second left, then left at lights and almost immediately right. Pick up signs for Portonuovo and Santiago and arrive at that great city in another 45 km.

• Through the Picos to the Monasterio de Santo Toribio.

Even for experienced mountaineers, used to the towering masses of the Alps or Andes, the Picos de Europa are a thrill. Tucked in behind Spain's northern coast, they rise in a dense mass of needle peaks, their bony-white limestone, usually snow-clad, gleaming over valleys so sheltered that Mediterranean plants can flourish.

In the 8thC, at Covadonga on the northern side of the range, the Christian leader Pelayo gained a surprise victory over the all-conquering Moors, becoming, for his pains, King of Asturias. His victory marked the start of Spain's centuries-long process of reconquest and Covadonga, unsurprisingly, is a key national shrine, with a national park attached. The peaks themselves never lose their power to surprise, rising to nearly 3,000 metres in a range that is scarcely 50 km long. Challenging and wonderful for walking and climbing, they are also a first-rate proposition for touring by car – with the one drawback that,

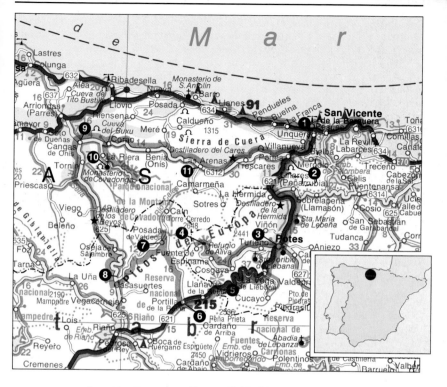

since the three massifs are divided by gorges that have no roads, you have to go the long way round. So much the better, if, as a result, you decide to linger on the way. That said, the only genuine problem is the weather, which is decidedly fickle. Do remember to take both rain gear and warm clothes for higher altitudes.

By the way, the Picos area also produces the strongest cheese in all Spain.

▬▬▬ ROUTE: 255 KM PLUS DETOURS

Llanes A serviceable seaside town, somewhat grey on weekdays, but festive at weekends, thanks to its position between sea and mountain, with excellent small beaches all along the coast and access to the Picos range behind. It makes a good start for this route, or indeed a base for walking the Picos. A tidal creek runs through the centre, serving as narrow port and focus for the town.

Gran Hotel An original resort hotel, about 100 years old, lovingly restored by local
Paraiso jeweller Antonio Ampudia Vega; accommodation is in apartments, with
(*hotel, Llanes*) mini-kitchens. *Calle Pidal 2; tel 98 540 04 82; closed mid-Oct to Easter;*
price band B.

El Riveru Asturian cider is poured from one hand held aloft into the thinnest of
(*restaurant* glasses held down low in the other hand. Resulting splashes are taken
and cider up by sawdust. Riveru specializes in anchovies, as well, along with more
house, Llanes) substantial fish dishes. Drink and food highly recommended. *Tel 98 540*
19 67; closed Mon and mid-Oct to mid-Dec; price band B.

*Leave town, heading east, for the N634. After 9 km, pause at Casa
Pancho (on the right hand side) in Vidiago.* Hung with a forest of hams
and home-made, spicy sausages, this traditional stopping-point of local
travellers also sells a full range of local cheeses, from the *fortissimo* blue
Cabrales (see below), to a milder local cows' cheese.

In Unquera, 24 km from Llanes, turn right ① for the Picos. The road
now runs up on the left bank of the River Deva, charming at this point,
with all manner of small craft, reaching Panes ② in 12 km. This drab
little spot is the real entry to the Picos, with a right turn here for
Cangas de Onis or straight on up for Potes. *Follow the Potes signs.* The
road soon enters the Hermidera gorge, winding tightly along the Deva
under precipitous cliff faces, trees clinging in extraordinary places, the
narrow strip of sky above sometimes alive with vultures and eagles.
Water runs on the rock faces, wild flowers proliferate and from the
crags above you begin to get some sense of the immensities of rock to
come.

*About 19 km from Panes, Lebeña is indicated, with left turn to Sta María
just after the bridge.* This small church, with a high mountain backdrop
and tender agricultural surroundings, is a near-perfect example of the
Mozarabic style, created by Christians moving north from Arab rule in
southern Spain, with Moorish features such as horseshoe arches and
abstract patterning. Not to be missed.

Back on the main road, gorge gives way to the wider valley of
Liebana. Suddenly the terrain is kinder, with vines and thoroughly
southern holm oak, wild olive and cistus. And rising above it all, to the
right, is the mountain wall of the eastern massif of the Picos. In front,
you begin to see the east-west range of the Cordillera Cantabrica.
In 9 km you reach Potes ③, capital of this part of the Picos. Here, there
is a range of eating places, bars and *churrerías*, hotels, pensions and
apartments, not to mention a castle, and a jolly holiday atmosphere at
weekends and in summer. But even better things await you on the
majestic detour into the mountains described below.

Fuente Dé *In the middle of Potes, leaving the castle on your right, head for Fuente Dé.*
(*48-km* *A short kilometre out of Potes, turn left.* In 3 km you reach the
detour) Monasterio de Santo Toribio (de Liebana), with fine views of the Picos

• *Farmer, Liebana valley.*

as you ascend. The much-rebuilt monastery has appealing features including a Romanesque doorway. In the monastery shop you can buy *orujo*, a fierce spirit made, like *marc* or *grappa*, from the leavings after wine-pressing. There is a hermitage a short way further up the road. Returning to the valley, the climb to Fuente Dé begins, still more or less following the River Deva. It is a temperate valley, with poplars, meadows and fruit trees, while the mountains, thrillingly acute, move in and out of view.

Approaching Fuente Dé, at Cosgaya you will see the stone of the Hotel del Oso, a little large for its setting, but a comfortable stopping place with easily the best restaurant locally. The speciality has to be attempted to be believed – a dish called *cocido lebaniego*, which features chick peas, cabbage, pork, veal, mountain ham, chorizo and pork lard with a topping that includes bread crumbs, eggs, parsley and, yes, *chorizo* once again. One portion will certainly do for two. *Address: Cosgaya, Cantabrica; tel 942 73 30 18; closed Jan 7 – Feb 15; price band B.*

The *oso* or Iberian brown bear features not only in this hotel's name but in local lore, since it was one of these which killed King Fáfila, successor of the victorious Pelayo who had gone on to found an

• *The church of Santa María de Lebeña.*

Asturian dynasty. The Oso Hotel has sundry representations of bears, but in fact the sharply dwindling bear population now lives almost entirely in the Reserva Nacional de Somiedo, south-west of Oviedo, the present-day Asturian capital.

Another 12 km or so brings you to ④ the high cliff amphitheatre at Fuente Dé, a sight worth travelling a great deal further for, and made still more intriguing by the knowledge that up behind there are more peaks, needles and truncated towers of rock, high among swirling clouds. From Fuente Dé, a cable car wings its way to the lip of the great cliff and for those with the time, the hardihood – and gear – there are splendid mountain walks up there.

Lying in alpine-style meadows beneath the cliff and the cable car is Parador Río Deva. Apart from its position, this is one of the most disappointing of the paradors, institutional in aspect and made rather shabby by the mountain climate. *Tel 942 73 00 01; closed Jan-Feb; price band B.*

Return to Potes, and turn sharp right, just before the Picos de Europa Hostal, for the Puerto de San Glorio. Though this is still notionally a national route, the N621, it becomes steep, narrow, tortuous – and demanding on the driver.. The compensation is a ravishing valley landscape, rising higher and higher. You pass villages in a vernacular architecture – rough stone, wide-spreading roofs – that appear to have grown out of the mountainside. Meadows tilt crazily, snow usually beckons.

At the Puerto de San Glorio ⑤ (1,609 metres and with fine views of the Cordillera Cantabrica to the south) either leave your car and walk, or bump another 2 km up the rough but passable track to the right to the Mirador de Llesba. Here you will find (200 metres above the road) a sad-faced monument to the bear and a glorious outlook over the Picos, for the first time fully revealing the saw-toothed central massif (left) as well as the jagged eastern (right). Though you may need your warm clothes, this is a fine spot for a picnic and a stroll.

The road continues (entering Castilla y León) through easier terrain and then, after Llanaves de la Reina, descends through a brief (granite) gorge. *At Portilla de la Reina ⑥, take the (still notional) N621 right for Sta Marina de Valdeón. Cross the Puerto de Pandetrave (1,562 metres)* and, immediately afterwards, pull up for astonishing views revealing the last of the central massif and the first spires and turrets of the western. From here, the road drops down into one of the best-loved valleys of the Picos, plunging between ever-rising needle-spires.

After picturesque Sta Marina (very rough surface in the village) the road suddenly becomes single track; passing other cars is a difficult manoeuvre. Eventually you drop down on to wider roads at Posada de Valdeón ⑦. Here you may well encounter buses, come to meet ramblers at the northern end of their walk through the spectacular Cares gorge which here runs right through the Picos, north to south.

• *Puente Romano, Cangas de Onis.*

Mirador del Tombo
(7-km detour)

If you have an appetite for more single-track road, you can penetrate even further down towards the Cares gorge by keeping right in Posada de Valdeón. Continue to Mirador del Tombo, only 800 metres in height, but with a formidable rockscape. There is even a small road which leads further still, as far as the gorge-mouth at Cain. It is clearly marked as dangerous, which does not deter some brave spirits.

From Posada de Valdeón, take the larger incoming road westwards. Climb, and climb, with magnificent viewpoints over the central and western massifs and crossing the Puerto de Panderrueda, after 10 km, at 1,450 metres. On meeting the N625, a further 5 km, turn right for Cangas de Onis, and climb to cross ⑧ the Puerto del Pontón. From here, the road descends to Cangas de Onis, where Pelayo set up his capital after the victory at Covadonga. The road runs down the western edge of the western massif, through the thrilling gorge of Los

• *Sacred cave of Pelayo, Covadonga.*

Beyos, following the River Sella.

Cangas de Onis

The little town of Cangas is effectively the capital of the western Picos. Just to your left as you meet the T-junction that signals arrival, there is a splendid medieval bridge across the Río Sella, known as the Puente Romano, with a replica of the Cross of Pelayo swinging beneath the arch.

Los Lagos
(hotel/ restaurant, Cangas de Onis)

A comfortable, modern hotel, with a restaurant and a cider bar attached. *Jardines del Ayuntamiento 3; tel 98 584 92 77; price band B.* ⑨ *From Cangas, take the C6312 in the direction of Panes along the northern side of the Picos.* The valley which the road now follows is divided from the coast by the high rock ridge of the Sierra de Cuera. With the Picos often visible to the south, this is one of the loveliest parts of the whole route.

Covadonga
(38-km detour)

Some 4 km from Cangas, turn right up an incoming valley floor for this unmissable detour. Tourist souvenir shops and huge parking lots soon reveal that an important site is imminent. The Covadonga complex ⑩, in 7 km, consists of a wide-mouthed cave in a rockface on the right-hand side of the valley, converted into an outdoor chapel and containing the 18thC Virgin of Battles – the original was accidentally burned; an immense basilica; a school; and a Civil Guards barracks. Most impressive, and most sacred, is the cave-chapel, reached either up

• *Monument to the bear, subject of local folklore, Mirador de Llesba.*

steep steps or by a tunnel from the upper car park. Pelayo's battle was supposedly fought on the precipitous hillsides opposite.

The Covadonga National Park is a chunk of land shaped like an axe-blade, its cutting edge deep in the mountains to the south. A mountain road, steep and sometimes exposed but travelled fearlessly by all comers, leads from Covadonga, 11 km up to a pair of high lakes, Enol and Ercina. Though some development has recently been taking place here, the views are inspirational.

Back on the C6312, continue along the valley to Ortiguero, after which, once again, you are in gorge territory. As the gorge ends, you enter the Cabrales region, home of the local blue cheese, on sale in most of the villages. It is supposedly composed of the 'three milks' of sheep, goat and cow, though one suspects that the proportion changes drastically with the seasons. What is certain is that the penicillin-style mould that gives the cheese its flavour occurs naturally in the local limestone caverns in which the cheeses are matured. The resulting product has a long-fought-for *denominación de origen* and a much-prized, if rather ugly, label.

Soon after Carreña de Cabrales, the viewing point on the right, the Pozo de la Oración or Well of Prayer, offers lovely views of Naranjo de Bulnes, the most striking peak in the central massif.

Principado de Europa
(*hotel/ restaurant, Póo de Cabrales*)

New and somewhat raw, but comfortable; good food, too. Sixteen rooms face on to a great mountain view and the young hotelier, Adolfo Nava, is a former mountain guide. *Tel 98 584 54 74; price band B.*

At Arenas de Cabrales ⑪ – more cheese, hotels and eating places – there is a right turn towards the mountains and the start of the Cares gorge walk (best avoided on Sundays and Bank Holidays); also to the high village of Sotres. The even higher village of Bulnes can be reached only by walking. Its fine cheeses come down on the backs of pack animals.

Carry on along the C6312, following the River Cares, 23 beautiful kilometres to Panes.

Casa Julian
(*hotel/ restaurant, Niserias*)

Some 15 km on from Arenas, you will find this salmon fisherman's delight: a charming restaurant and hotel with the perhaps dubious distinction of having been used regularly for his siesta, during annual fishing holidays, by the late General Franco.

Hotel and dining-room hang over the river. On the far side of the road there is an annexe and a bar, selling not only the local *orujo* but salmon flies. Salmon is the top dish; other specialities include clams with *fabes*, the white beans much prized in Asturias, also oven-baked lamb. *Tel 98 541 41 79; closed late Oct to mid-March; hotel price band A, restaurant price band A/B.*

You are soon back in Panes. Retrace on the road to Unquera, or continue 12 km east, over beautiful rising ground, to come down at San Vicente de la Barquera to a wide estuary. The historic little town stands mostly on a promontory between the two river mouths within the estuary, showing an intriguing profile of church and castle: water, boats and all that goes with them – a delightful spot to end a tour.

• *The rooftops of Frias, with the Ebro valley below.*

Haro is wine capital of La Rioja, most famous of Spain's wine-producing districts. It is also an excellent point of access for the region generally and this soon proves to be about a good deal more than wine. The Ebro, running down diagonally from north-west to south-east, has always been a means of passage across Spain, from Arab raiders working northwards to travellers on more peaceable missions. The region is also crossed diagonally, this time from the north-east, by the greatest Pilgrims' Way of Europe, the Camino de Santiago or Road of St James. Hugely rich in monuments as a result, the Rioja's history as a through-way is reflected in an easy temperament, matched by an abundance of Spain's best food, including quite outstanding vegetables. The landscape is beautiful and varied, from river valley to imposing mountain. The first of our loops sticks to the Rioja proper, crossing the Camino de Santiago at two crucial points. But as a reminder of the harsh country the Ebro has passed through before arrival, the second route plunges back north-west into gorge terrain, visiting a corner of the Basque Country and rather more of historic Castile.

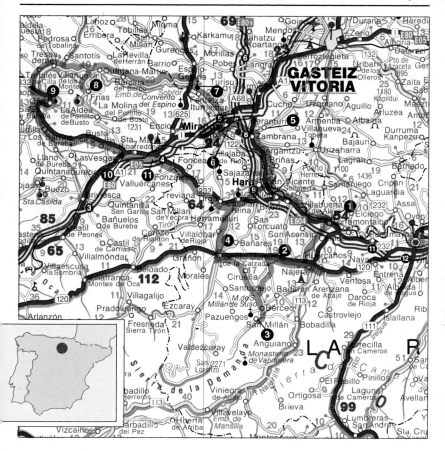

■ ROUTE ONE: 76 KM

Haro

Haro flows down from its hilltop, close to Las Conchas de Haro, the dramatic limestone 'gate' that admits the Ebro to the Rioja. The town itself is a mix of elegant and scruffy. Make your way to the centre, the delightful Plaza de la Paz, with its fine 18thC own hall, arcades and bandstand and a handsome palace with bars and cafés along its base. Then stroll up to the church of Santo Tomás, the local landmark, with a grand plateresque doorway. Down in the lower part of town, mostly round the railway station, a great many *bodegas* (wineries), are clustered, ranging from Federico Paternina to López de Heredia. Best time to try for a visit is round 11 am, with López de Heredia the most agreeably old-fashioned, Muga the more welcoming.

• *Plaza de la Paz, Haro.*

Beethoven II and Terete
(*restaurants, Haro*)

Beethoven II, with its somewhat bourgeois air of comfort, is a good place to make a start on such typical Riojan dishes as *menestra de verdura*, mixed vegetables, usually with artichokes, asparagus, beans and peas. Grilled fish and lamb are also favoured. *C/ Santo Tomás; tel 941 31 11 81; closed Mon eve and all day Tues; price band B.* Your wine, of course, must be a Rioja, perhaps a dark and velvety red, tasting of vanilla after maturing in American oak barrels.

The Terete specializes in oven-roast lamb and has a cellar to thrill – 250,000 bottles in a medieval tunnel in the rock and a grand hall of barrels, one containing 16,000 litres; *Lucrecia Arena 17; tel 941 31 00 23; closed Sun night and Mon; price band B.*

• *Tracery in the cloister archway of Santa María la Real, Nájera.*

Los Agustinos
(hotel, Haro)

A palatial building arranged round a stern cloister. Beginning as a convent, it has also done time as a prison – prisoners' graffiti are scratched into the cloister columns. Solid comfort. *San Agustín 2; tel 941 31 13 08/31 15 62); price band C.*

Leave the Plaza de la Paz on the right (as you must) and pick up signs for Logroño. Reaching the N232, follow right for 7 km towards Logroño. On your left, the gaunt limestone wall that guards the Rioja rears impressively, with the Ebro valley in between, its eminences marked by ancient villages. Grapes grow in relatively small vineyards, interspersed with wheat and other crops. It is a fitting first taste of the beauties of the Rioja.

Briones

In this ancient village, wine is sold from private houses. The Calle Mayor has faded escutcheons and massive wooden doors with heavy decorative studs in metal.
Continue 4 km on the N232, then ① turn right for San Asensio just before the Afersa wine cooperative. Angle right to pass through the village. Here the well-known rosé wines of the locality are sold from cooperatives as well as from houses.

Najera

Back on the through-road, continue about 8 km, passing poplars, vines and grassy tummocks to the N120. Turn left and very shortly right for Najera Oeste (Najera West), running in under a strange red cliff cut through the sandstone hills by the River Najerilla.

• *Sheep grazing near San Millán de la Cogolla.*

Pocked with caves, it is no surprise that Najera became a burial place for the kings of Navarre and featured on the Camino de Santiago. As so often, the scrap of surviving old town clusters round the bridge, with Santa María la Real as the main pilgrimage centre. There's a 16thC cloister with different, and sumptuous tracery in each of its 24 arches, and the church beyond is really an extension outwards of the cave that contained the royal tombs. After many sackings, most of these are substitutes, but in the church you will find the 12thC Romanesque coffin lid of Doña Blanca of Navarre, expressively crowded with small-scale scenes and figures.

Los Parrales
(*restaurant, Najera*)

Los Parrales occupies a pretty first floor above the bar, overlooking the river. The Villoslada family serve their Riojan specialities – *alubias blancas con almejas* (white beans with clams) or *patatas con chorizo* (potatoes with home-made, paprika-flavoured sausage) along with more standard restaurant fare. *C/ Mayor 52; tel 941 36 37 30; closed Mon night in winter; price band B.*

For those who want to stay over, there's a slightly utilitarian hotel, the San Fernando, *tel 941 36 37 00, price band A.*

San Millán de la Cogolla

San Millán lies south of the main Camino de Santiago, but is much visited by pilgrims. For the most direct approach (there are also more discursive routes through mountain country), *return to the N120 and turn back left along it. After 7 km, ② turn left for San Millán and travel another 10 km, through glorious, rising country, facing south into the Sierra de la Demanda.* The peak in front of you, often snow-covered into June, is San Lorenzo.

Stop off on the way at the noble 13thC Cistercian abbey of Cañas. San Millán himself was one of Spain's early holy men, living in the Visigothic 5thC, and is held responsible for a host of miracles. The church around his original hermitage is a real rarity, with two naves built crankily along the cliff-face, high among woods and rocks. It contains a plethora of horse-shoe arches and other intriguing details of the Visigothic, Mozarabic and Romanesque periods, as well as San Millán's fine alabaster tomb. This is the Monasterio de Suso or Up Above (well signposted). Later the monks moved down into the valley and built themselves the massive Monasterio de Yuso or Down Below. This possessed, in the form of a marginal notation on parchment, the first known text written in Castilian together with the first written example of the far older Basque language. This gives San Millán a key position in the history of language.

Monks lead conducted tours in the lower monastery. With mixed woodland, soft valleys and mountains above, this is one of the most idyllic spots in north-eastern Spain, with good walking in the vicinity.

Santo Domingo de la Calzada

Leave San Millán on the main approach road through ③ Berceo (birthplace of the first Castilian poet), then follow signs on minor roads to Santo Domingo de la Calzada (Saint Dominic of the Causeway), 16 beautiful, rolling kilometres. Meeting the N120 in Santo Domingo, turn left ④ into town then obliquely right for the cathedral and park as you can. (You may be forced into a right turn that actually runs through the cathedral porch, not exactly a triumph of town planning).

Santo Domingo built a causeway for the pilgrims over the River Oja – the stream which gives its name to the Rioja. He lived to a great age and became the patron of bridge-builders, highway construction engineers, the Spanish Society of Gerontology and other related causes. His tomb is in the cathedral. There is also a carved wooden gallery containing a live cock and hen. The story goes that a serving maid in the local inn fell in love with a handsome young German pilgrim. When he spurned her advances, she loaded his knapsack with the hotel silver. He was caught and hanged, but weeks later, when his parents passed the gibbet on their return from Santiago, they found their son was still alive. They burst in to tell the judge, who was engaged on a chicken dinner. "If it's true", he said, "these birds on my plate will crow". And so they did. The boy was freed and a cock and hen have been kept in the cathedral ever since.

Parador de Santo Domingo
(hotel, Santo Domingo)

The inn which features in the tale above happens to be the newly refurbished Parador de Santo Domingo de la Calzada, just across from the cathedral, *tel 941 34 03 00, price band C.* Good restaurant, *price band B/C.* For cheaper, hearty eating, try the pilgrim-friendly Hidalgo, *c/ Hilario Pérez 10, on the first floor, tel 941 34 02 27; price band A.*
④ *Head back east on N120 to pick up signs, well within town, for Haro then continue 20 km north across the flat valley, saving Casalarreina for another occasion.*

■■■■ ROUTE TWO: 182 KM

Longer than Route One, this loop follows a circle which is not easy to break because of the nature of the terrain; also, some of the most interesting spots are at its furthest extreme. In the early stages, you will encounter modern industry as well as impressive landscape and soon after that a nuclear power station: not to everyone's taste, but the route is well known to Spaniards, and much appreciated by them, since it runs through one of the finest gorges in the whole gorge-ridden course of the upper Ebro and visits Frías and Oña, two small towns with a great weight of history.

Begin by taking the N232 north from Haro, through the natural limestone gate of las Conchas de Haro and so into a corner of the Basque country. ⑤ One km after Zambrana, follow signs left for industrial Miranda de Ebro, tucked into a corner of Castile.

Miranda de Ebro

Signs for 'centro ciudad' and then 'casco antiguo' lead through a drab town to an ancient river crossing. It's worth a quick stop in the old town here, or a slow one for a meal.

Vasca
(*restaurant, Miranda de Ebro*)

In the old town. Waitresses in old-fashioned black dresses bring forth brimming dishes of Iberian jamón and groaning platters of asparagus and chops. Red wine comes chilled and small children nestle in grandparents' arms. *First floor at C/ Olmo 3; tel 947 31 13 01; closed Sun night; price band A/B.*

   To get out of Miranda and back on the route, continue over the bridge, with signs for Hospital Oron. ⑥ Reaching the N1, double back over the Ebro and soon turn left (C122), signposted for Puentelarra and the A1 Autopista. Ignoring the motorway entrance, cross back into the Basque Country, running north past factories and into gathering countryside. Fontecha has a pretty little castle.

Reaching the A2625, about 13 km from Miranda, keep right for Bilbao and Orduña, then ⑦ shortly turn left across the River Ormecillo, signposted for Sobrón (5 km) and Trespaderne (32 km). You are approaching a major gorge – and a major source of electricity.

Sobrón Gorge

The gorge leads westward, into the Castilian province of Burgos. It opens with electricity sub-stations, but the pylons soon become invisible, thanks to the cliffs. You are left alone with the road, with cyclists training hard and fishermen taking it easy. Sometimes the upper limestone cliffs are fluted, organ-like. Sometimes they rise in spear-like pinnacles. Sometimes the crags look just like castles. The road, though good enough, winds fiercely: griffon vultures loom above, huge in silhouette. The river is no less beautiful after the point where it is

• *Frías's medieval bridge.*

dammed to form the Sobrón Reservoir.

Finally, the gorge runs out into the wider valley of Tobalina and here the anticipated nuclear power station rises as a harsh grey block, then falls away behind. The route continues through spectacular scenery.

Frías

This is the next major sight, rising as a honey-coloured hump of stone on a hump of hill within the broadening Ebro valley. *Soon after the village of Quintana Martín Galindez, ⑧ take an unexpected hill-top, turning left 4 km to Frías. The road crosses the Ebro parallel to a lovely medieval bridge.*

Frías is a special place. As you climb towards the crag you begin to realize that the top-most tower of the castle – originally Romanesque, refashioned by Alfonso VIII (1158-1214) – is built on a fang of rock which appears to lean sharply outwards over the little town beneath. Leaving your car on entry, walk up a narrow street, flanked by half-timbered houses (there are several eating places) to a narrow promontory with town hall, church and castle. Climbing the castle's tower on its leaning rock, you are rewarded by fine views of the roofscape below and a teasing sense of insecurity.

Return over the river to the road from which you have temporarily diverted, and on to Trespaderne. Here turn left ⑨ along the N629, through yet more thrilling gorge country, for Oña. After about 7 km, turn left again at the T-junction with the N232, and arrive in a further 5 km, at Oña, going through a very narrow limestone gateway on the way.

• *A street in Frías, with the castle in the background.*

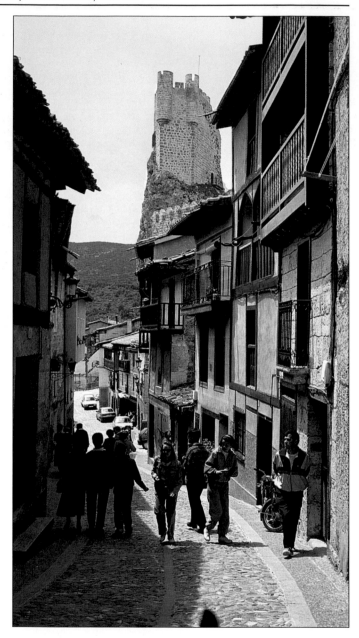

Oña

As seat of many of the early Counts of Castile, whose descendants became the rulers of a greater Spain, Oña has a firm place in Spanish history. The great monastery of San Salvador is now a mental hospital and cannot be visited, but there are intriguing prospects of changing levels, pleasant plazas, old streets and valiantly surviving churches.

Hostal Morales
(*restaurant, Oña*)

The modest Hostal Morales offers a solidly good lunch for travellers, eaten under the stuffed heads of wild boar, wolf and many pairs of antlers. There are simple rooms, no private bathrooms. *On the main road just opposite the Repsol garage; tel. 947 30 00 73; price band A.*

From Oña. run down out of the hills, still following the very rural N232, with the limestone ridge (through which the last gorge led) soon rising to your left. Away to the right, over the broad and lovely valley, there are views once again of the Sierra de la Demanda. The N232 joins the N1 ⑩ for a stretch near Pancorbo and then continues east. (If, however, you continue on the N1 you will almost immediately enter ⑪ the famous Pancorbo gorge, which will seem child's play compared to those you have already seen. There are hotels on the north side of the gorge, and a scatter of hostales to the south.)

The N232 continues to Haro from Pancorbo, running into the Rioja through halcyon countryside. You cross the Oja at Casalarreina with the possibility of an interesting stop. The monastery church of Nuestra Señora de la Piedad has a fine doorway; the Palacio de los Condestables on the other side of the main road is in a sad state of ruin.

And so back to Haro, entering by the same road as Route One.

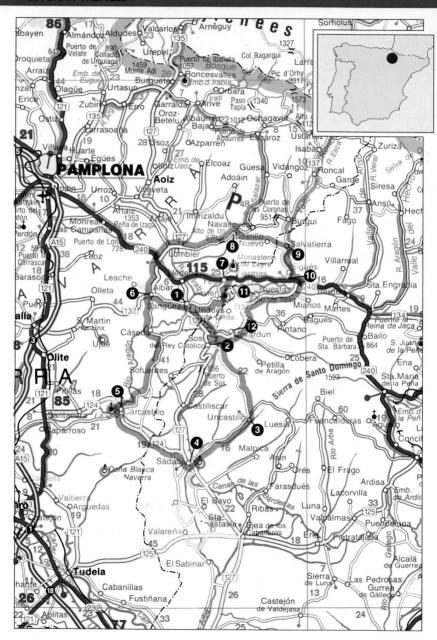

• *Lunar-like landscape, near Ruesta.*

Since the order of St James was founded at Santiago de Compostela in the Middle Ages, this area, on the Aragon-Navarre borders, has been a focal point for pilgrims on the long trek across the Pyrenees from France to Galicia. They still come in their hundreds, in May and June, in time for the Feast of St James on July 25, laden with rucksacks and carrying a staff and cross as well as the cockle shells that are the symbol of St James. They pass through a landscape of wonderful variety, winding down through the foothills of the Pyrenees and across the arid plains of Aragon. Many use Sangüesa, the meeting point of these two loops, as a stopping place.

The two loops offer total contrasts in scenery. The first explores the plain, along with some historical sights, including three of las Cinco Villas or 'The Five Towns'. None is larger than a village, but they were raised to the status of town for the support they gave Philip V in the War of Succession at the beginning of the 18thC.

The second loop focuses on the dramatic natural beauty of the foothills. Restaurants are few and far between, so buy picnic ingredients before leaving Sangüesa. You'll also find it rewarding to take a field guide to help identify the incredible variety of wild flowers and birds.

■■■■■■ ROUTE ONE: 110 KM

Sangüesa
This quiet agricultural town beside the Rio Aragon was, and still is, an important stopping place on the pilgrim trail to Santiago de Compostela. Its five churches tell of its early importance – the best of them, Santa Maria, beside the Aragon, has a magnificent portal showing the apostles, including Judas Iscariot grotesquely hanging from a rope. There are some splendid houses, most notably the Baroque Palacio de Vallesantoro and the porticoed *ayuntamiento*, which leads to what remains of the castle.

  The modestly priced Pension Las Navas offers the only accommodation in the town centre; the two-star Yamaguchi, more comfortable but twice the cost, is not far out of town.
① *Leave the centre, following the signs for Sos del Rey Católico. The road runs straight as a die south-east over the plain, crossing first the Rio Onsella and then the Canal de Las Bardenas before winding uphill into Sos, lying at the edge of the Sierra de Peña.*

Sos del Rey Católico
A picturesque mountain village and the most outstanding of las Cinco Villas, Sos was the birthplace in 1452 of Ferdinand of Aragon, the first ruler of a united Spain. Lose yourself here for a while and enjoy the medieval atmosphere, wandering the narrow cobbled streets within the defensive walls. You pass grand mansions with carved timber eaves, doorways and balconies on the climb to the castle remains which look out over mottled pink roofs to the plain. The church, just below the castle, has an interesting crypt, traces of frescos and carved choir stalls.

Parador Fernando de Aragon
(hotel, Sos)
Although this is a modern parador on the edge of the village, it blends in well with its medieval surroundings. Spacious and comfortably furnished, it makes a pricier but more luxurious alternative to staying at Sangüesa. The restaurant has superb views across the plains to the conical Monte de Tabar. The food is excellent: try the *conejo guisado a la cazadora* – rabbit stewed with mushrooms, onion and wine. *Tel 948 88 80 11; price band B.*

② *On the outskirts of Sos, fork left for Uncastillo. The road winds across the Sierra de Peña and at its highest point you have views of the snow-capped Pyrenees in the distance. There are few, if any, cars. Practically every centimetre of this 22 km stretch is lined with bright red poppies in summer.*

Uncastillo
The village, another of las Cinco Villas, suddenly appears before you, its honey-coloured medieval houses guarded by the remains of an impressive 13thC castle standing on a lofty perch. The Romanesque church of Santa Maria is worth a closer look, not only for its unusual turreted and pinnacled tower which wouldn't appear out of place on a

• *Coat of arms decorating an Aibar house.*

fairy-tale castle, but also for its beautifully sculpted south portal. Look closely and you'll see a few impudent faces being pulled. Another church, San Juan, has some well preserved 13thC frescos.

③ *Leave the village following the signs for Sábada along the Rio Riguel, which has gouged a mini canyon through the valley.* The road passes the little village of Layana, on a hillock and overlooked by a tower rent open to the sky on two sides. A signposted track leads from here to the remains of a Roman aqueduct and baths at Los Bañales.

Sábada The third and last of las Cinco Villas to be seen on this route, Sábada is far less attractive than either Sos del Rey Católico or Uncastillo. Its most obvious feature is the massive square blockhouse of a castle, complete with towers, and some major cracks in its walls. It can only be viewed externally. Less obvious is the tomb of a 2ndC Roman family, signposted down a track just before you reach the village. In the village itself, pollarded lime trees provide riverside shade, where old men sit to chat and smoke or just watch the world go by.

④ *Follow the signs for Sos del Rey Católico through Sábada and after crossing the river turn left opposite a petrol station in the direction of Carcastillo.* The road now heads across a parched and rugged plain where a few farmers try to scratch a living. You pass Alera, a modern village development, surrounded by trees like an oasis.

• *Monasterio de Leyre, haven of pilgrims en route to Santiago de Compostela.*

⑤ *At the crossroads in the centre of Carcastillo, a modern-looking and uninteresting agricultural town, turn left for Caparroso and almost immediately left again for the Monasterio de la Oliva, reached in 2.5 km.*

Monasterio de la Oliva   Approached by a tree-lined road through fields of cereals and vines, the monastery provides a welcome and cool retreat from the heat of the day. The simple 12thC Cistercian church is thought to be the oldest example of Gothic architecture in Spain, while the cloisters display some beautifully sculptured tracery and intricate floor designs. *Retrace to Carcastillo and at the central crossroads continue in the direction of Cáseda and Sangüesa, climbing at first and then descending a wooded hill to the plain. Take your time: there are some wonderful views.*

Cáseda   A medieval hill village beside the Rio Aragon. There is little to keep you here other than some picturesque balconied houses bedecked in flowers. More cats than people seem to wander the streets – the locals are more likely to be found in one of the bars, arguing noisily or playing cards. There are some pleasant shady picnic spots down by the river, fountains included.

Continue across the plain to Aibar, another hill village with arcaded streets and fine views from the church terrace. ⑥ Turn right at the foot of the village and return to Sangüesa.

If you have time to spare, the following detour, 32 km return, is an interesting extra option. It also offers hotel alternatives. *From the centre of Sangüesa, follow the signs for Javier.*

Javier
(detour)

One of the holy sites on the pilgrim route, Javier was the birthplace, in 1506, of St Francis de Javier, a co-founder of the Jesuit Order. A well restored battlemented castle dating from the 11thC is now a museum to the saint's life and includes a chapel with a Dance of Death fresco. The adjoining Baroque church looks strangely out of place.

Xavier
(hotel/ restaurant, Javier)

This hotel, among trees just across the road from the castle, was upgraded a couple of years ago and is now beautifully appointed, with comfortable rooms and polished wooden floors throughout. Prices are reasonable, even more so in the restaurant. *Tel 948 88 40 06; price band A.* The nearby Hotel El Meson is slightly cheaper.

Beyond Javier, the road drops down into the Aragon valley, crossing the river just before Yesa, while ahead, the Sierra de Leyre rises like a wall. As you cross the river look left and you'll see the remains of a medieval bridge, which would have been the ancient link between the Monasterio de Leyre and Javier.
⑦ *Turn left at Yesa and just through the village (there are a couple of modestly priced restaurants here) turn right for the Monasterio de Leyre, reached in about 4 km along a twisting, climbing road.*

Monasterio de Leyre

High in the Pyrenean foothills, this Romanesque monastery has been a pilgrim-haven for hundreds of years, and they still stop at the small hotel here, en route for Santiago de Compostela. Only part of the monastery is open to the public – the church where, several times a day, you can hear the Gregorian chants of the Benedictine monks, and the 9thC crypt, with its forest of stumpy columns topped by huge capitals, and a chest containing the remains of Navarre's earliest kings. The views are magnificent.

Hospederla de Leyre
(hotel, Leyre)

Worldly comforts are available for travellers of all kinds in this two-star rated hotel attached to the monastery. Rooms are simply furnished but reasonably priced and there is a good restaurant and bar. *Tel 948 88 41 00; price band A.*

Retrace to Yesa and then to Sangüesa.

• *Hoz de Esca.*

■■■■■■■ ROUTE TWO: 109 KM

Leave Sangüesa by the bridge over the Rio Aragon and immediately turn left in the direction of Aibar. After 8 km you arrive at Aibar. ⑥ Turn right in the direction of Lumbier and climb grassy hills to the Aibar Pass before dropping down the far side towards the main Pamplona-Huesca road. Take your time on the way down: the views are wonderful. Cross the main road and in a couple of kilometres turn right into Lumbier, but instead of bearing left into the village, continue to the right towards the Hoz de Lumbier.

Hoz de Lumbier
(detour)

Although you can drive along a track into this amazing gorge, it is better to leave the car at the entrance and walk in, through a 200-m tunnel and alongside the tumbling green waters of the Rio Irati. The path, which follows a former railway line, continues 5 km to the N240 near Liédena. You'll find one or two picnic places along the way – though for company you'll have eagles circling overhead watching for a bite to eat. *Return to Lumbier.*

Lumbier

Ignore the modern development at the edge of the village: the centre is charming. Parking may be a problem but continue to the end of the Calle Mayor and you should find a space. The 14thC Church of the Asunción at the back of the Plaza de Las Fueros is worth seeing for its huge and intricate gilt altarpiece and its statuary, and if you feel like a cooling drink or a *bocadillo*, there are several bars nearby, the Bar Torres undoubtedly being the liveliest.

From Lumbier, head towards Navascués, driving at first along the edge of the plain and then after Domeño winding and climbing through wilder country to the Iso Pass.

Hoz de Arbayun

The second gorge of the day is even more spectacular than the first. Although you can't enter, as you could the Hoz de Lumbier, you can look down into it from a dizzily perched observation platform. Ochre-streaked limestone cliffs plunge to the river below, while high above the rim eagles and vultures circle lazily. Even in June you could be here alone, with only the sound of water and birdsong.

The road winds downhill for two or three kilometers, then just after passing an old bridge across the Rio Salazar, turn right in the direction of Bigüezal and Castillo Nuevo ⑧. The riverside beside the new bridge provides an attractive picnic spot.

Every bend in the road now brings a new mountain spectacle. Bigüezal, a tiny whitewashed village with a big square, sits on a terrace on the hillside, then, beyond, the views to the Pyrenees' higher peaks more than make up for the deteriorating road surface.

This village of steep, narrow streets and attractive whitewashed houses wouldn't look out of place on one of the *costas* – minus the tourists and souvenirs, of course. If you can struggle on up the steep paths to the church, there are views down the valley.

Castillo Nuevo

The 5 km from Castillo Nuevo to Salvatierra de Esca requires careful driving. The road is poorly surfaced, narrow and winding, and there is no protection against the big drop to the right. The scenery is superb. ⑨ *At the T-junction turn left into Salvatierra.*

Salvatierra de Esca

Attractively located at the northern end of the Hoz de Esca, Salvatierra stands on a hilltop in wild countryside. Just below the village is another riverside picnic spot and a chance for a cooling paddle.

From Salvatierra return to the T-junction, then head south through the Hoz de Esca. This is another outstanding gorge with the Rio Esca winding along beside the road, deep and narrow enough to block most sunlight apart from around midday.

Sigüés

A sleepy village at the other end of the Hoz de Esca, Sigüés has a pretty little 12thC Romanesque church with an arcaded entrance. Note also the strange pepperpot style chimneys on several of the houses. An unusual modern sculpture, erected in 1988 in the Plaza de Aragon, depicts a man standing on a raft of logs.

Continue south for about 3 km to the N 240, turn left for Huesca ⑩, *then in another 3 km turn right towards Sos del Rey Católico* ⑪. The road passes a strangely eroded, lunar landscape, then shortly afterwards superb views of the Embalse de Yesa open out. There are several excellent picnic spots here.

Embalse de Yesa

This man-made lake was formed in 1959 when the Rio Aragon was dammed to help supply water to the area. Around 14 km long and more than 2 km wide, its turquoise water is a significant feature of the landscape, an attraction for visitors with its possibilities for fishing and sailing, but a blight for farmers, many of whom have lost land. Recent plans to increase the capacity of the lake have led to a campaign in which the daubed protests on walls are strangely contradictory to British eyes – 'Yesa-No'.

Ruesta

Whole communities lost their homes when Yesa was created and one such is Ruesta, which stands at a point where the road turns away from the lake. At first you see its castle standing in ruins on the hilltop, then you see the church and its houses huddled around. But as you approach you realize that this village is even quieter than usual and that the whole place is in ruins. It comes as a shock if you're not expecting it, but the stillness has a certain beauty.

• Unusual
modern
sculpture, Plaza
de Aragon,
Sigüés.

Beyond Ruesta, the road winds along a valley, then climbs to the Puerto de
Cuatro Caminos, where there are more opportunities to pull off the road for
a picnic. Farther on, the road descends into another valley, passing
villages such as Urriés and Navardún where a tower standing on a
hillock is all that remains of the castle.

After Navardún bear right for Sos after crossing the Rio Onsella, reaching
Sos in 8 km. From Sos, return to Sangüesa over the plain.

• *Abizanda.*

Most roads through the Pyrenees follow the valleys running from north to south, so this route abandons our usual figure-of-eight format. It's a linear route worth doing in its own right, but it also makes an interesting way to round off a visit to Spain if you are returning northwards.

Some of the north-south roads through the mountains stop short of the high Pyrenees; others go on to cross the frontier into France using minor passes. This route does the latter, giving you the chance to explore unspoiled mountain landscapes and delightful towns and villages and to avoid the frantic, often congested border crossings of Irun and La Jonquera.

Starting at Barbastro, you head north past the turquoise lakes of the Cinca Valley, heading initially for Bielsa and its tunnel border crossing. However, at Ainsa you branch off into the Ara Valley, towards the most beautiful of the Pyrenees' two national parks, the Ordesa, where the marvellous walking and superb scenery may delay you a while. At Biescas, you turn north again, this time into the Gállego Valley, which takes you, by way of a detour to the fascinating old spa resort of Balneario de Panticosa, to the frontier.

The views going back to Barbastro are completely different, so don't regard this journey as strictly one way: it's just as satisfying as a drive into the mountains and back again.

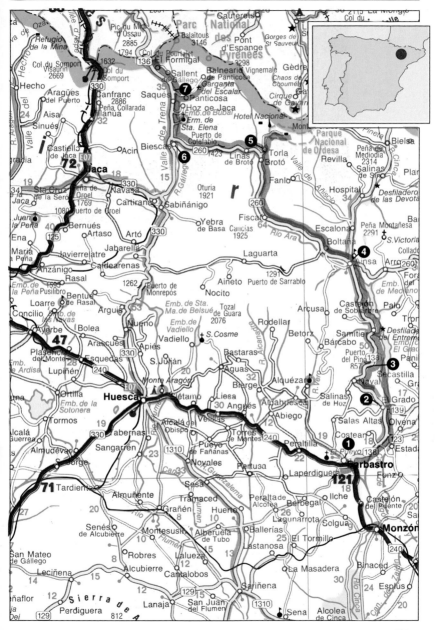

• *Cloisters of Ainsa's 12thC Romanesque church.*

ROUTE: 147 KM

Barbastro

Barbastro stands on a major route across the Pyrenees from the Mediterranean to the Bay of Biscay. It is an unattractive town, but the brick-built 16thC cathedral with its separate tower is worth a visit to admire the outstanding interior, which includes an impressive alabaster retable by Damián Forment and an intricately vaulted chapel. If you want to stay in the town, try the modestly priced San Ramon Hotel, conveniently located in the centre.

Leave Barbastro ① following the signs for Francia and Ainsa. The road winds along the Rio Cinca to the foot of the dam at the southern end of the Embalse de El Grado, where you have a choice of routes. Some years ago there was no choice and the road went via El Grado and Naval to Abizanda; now a new road goes straight through to Abizanda. Take the new road if you want superb views of the turquoise coloured lake, the old one if you would prefer to visit the villages of El Grado and Naval. The way to El Grado and Naval is signposted, ② near the dam. If you're following the new road, you can see, on the far side of the lake, the Torreciudad sanctuary, built in 1975 by the mysterious Opus Dei sect, which includes flagellation among its medieval rites.

El Grado

This village, standing on a promontory overlooking the valley below the lake, has a picturesque if somewhat crumbling Calle Mayor, where the houses' balconies are draped with flowers. Follow the street down and you come to the 15thC brick-built collegiate church.
Continue on the winding road to Naval

Naval

Noted for its ceramics and pottery workshops where you can browse or buy, Naval stands on a hill topped by a lovely 16thC church. The exterior of brick and pink stone, has been well restored. The roof vaulting is unusual and the side chapels display interesting styles in ceiling design, sculptured arches and statuary. Sit there and enjoy the cool temperature – also the complete silence.
Continue to Abizanda, which lies off to the right. If you use the new road, turn left just after passing the village on its rocky perch.

Abizanda

Spectacularly sited where the old road rejoins the new, and best seen from the new road, Abizanda is totally agricultural, with little to show, other than the 11thC watchtower and a crumbling church totally dominating the village. Only about 15 people live here, but drive into the centre and someone is certain to appear to lead you up to the recently restored tower, complete with timber walkways, for a personal guided tour.
After leaving Abizanda turn right and at the new road ③ turn left, heading for Ainsa. There are occasional glimpses of the Embalse de El Grado and the Embalse de Mediano which follows it, along with several villages abandoned when the lakes were formed. One of them, Morillo de Tou, has since been restored and is now a holiday centre, complete with cottages and a camp site.

Ainsa

Driving into Ainsa you suspect that it is no more than a modern, uninteresting town of the southern Pyrenees. But there is much more to it than that: just follow the signs to the Casco Antiguo. The road winds up the hillside and before long you arrive in the large cobbled Plaza Mayor, three sides enclosed by the *ayuntamiento* and terraces of arcaded houses, the fourth open to the castle walls a little farther along the promontory. In one corner stands the 12thC Romanesque church with its pretty little crypt and triangular cloisters entered beneath the clocktower. Quiet during the day, the delightful square becomes animated when the locals take their evening *paseo*. A millenium ago, Ainsa was an important city, the capital of the Kingdom of Sobrarbe. A major battle was fought here against the Moors. The Christians were facing defeat when they had a vision of a cross in a tree and rallied, fighting on to victory. The event is celebrated in September every other year (1993, 1995 and so on) when the citizens dress up as Moors and Christians and re-enact the battle in the square.

Pirineos
(hotel, Ainsa)

Ainsa's *casco antiguo* has no hotels, but this easily spotted pink building in the modern town is within ten minutes' walk. With two stars, it is comfortable and reasonably priced, especially outside the peak season of July and August. It has a restaurant, but there are more romantic ones in the old town. *Tel 974 50 00 08; price band C.* There are several other hotels: perhaps the Dos Rios, just around the corner from the Pirineos, is one of the most recommendable; *price band B.*

Bodegas del Sobrarbe
(restaurant, Ainsa)

If you want a restaurant with a medieval atmosphere seek out this one, tucked away in a corner of the Plaza Mayor. The ground floor bar is somewhat contrived, with stained glass windows depicting the major protagonists in the town's famous battle, but the restaurant in the 11thC cellars effectively sets the mood. *Tel 974 50 02 37; price band A.* The Casa Albas at the opposite end of the square is a little more relaxed and marginally cheaper.

④, *From the crossroads at the centre of Ainsa, head in the direction of Broto.*

Boltaña

You could be understood for driving straight past Boltaña; but pull off to the right as you go through the lower modern part and drive up to the old hill-top village, parking by the church. The building, which dates from 1544, looks a mess outside, but inside it is perfectly ordered, with magnificent roof vaulting and beautifully carved choir stalls. Nearby, paved lanes lead into some delightful old courtyards.

Continue in the direction of Broto, soon reaching the Garganta de Jánovas, an impressive defile of the Rio Ara with incredible razor-edged vertical striations in the rocks. Beyond the gorge several villages lie abandoned and in ruins. Farther on, beyond Fiscal, the road passes along a wide, gentler valley full of wild flowers, the snow-capped Pyrenees growing ever closer.

Broto

A pretty village just off the road, and a useful place to stay in: there are several modestly priced hotels, among them the Mirador, *tel 974 48 61 77* and the Pradas, *tel 974 48 60 04.*

The road winds steeply up from Broto. Shortly you come to ⑤, *a turning right signposted Torla.*

• *Ainsa.*

Torla
(detour)

This simple grey stone mountain village is the main resort in this part of the Pyrenees, largely because of its proximity to the Ordesa National Park, one of the most outstanding national parks in Spain. It has a delightful location in the steep-sided Ara Valley with the peak of Mondarruego looking down from the valley head. Out of season it is charming and there is a choice of places to stay. In late July and August it can be unbearably crowded. If you need maps for exploring Ordesa, you'll find them here.

Viñamala
(hotel, Torla)

Right in the centre, this is a modern and well-appointed hotel with some wonderful views along the valley. Some rooms have balconies to take advantage of those views and there is a swimming pool if you need to cool off after a day hiking in the mountains. Prices are moderate, while a meal in the restaurant falls in price band A. *Tel 974 48 62 90.*

Ordesa National Park

The entrance to the park is some 8 km up the Ara Valley, where the road ends at a large car park among the trees. An information centre tells you about the area's rich flora and fauna. Make sure you have adequate footwear: there are endless waymarked paths along the lush canyon floor beside the foaming Rio Arazas. It's a popular place, understandably so with its grandiose scenery, the canyon walls rising hundreds of feet and spectacular waterfalls. If you can devote a day to walking here you will find solitude – most of the visitors never wander far from their cars.

**La Pradera
de Ordesa**
(*restaurant,
Ordesa*)

This simple place beside the car park is handy for a snack or for a three-course meal. It is open 9 am to 11 pm every day of the year, come 'rain, shine, little snow or lot of snow'. *Tel 974 48 60 82; price band A.*

Return to Torla and then to point ⑤, where turn right towards Biescas. This is a spectacular road, winding and climbing along the edge of a ravine. Soon after you start, look back and you'll have an outstanding view of Broto down in the valley.

**Linas de
Broto**

This mountain village with its pretty 12thC church is a popular place for hikers and has several bars, restaurants and places to stay at including the friendly and moderately priced Hostal Jal. Run by José and Josefa Pardo Allué, the Jal has the true look of a mountain inn, with hiking sticks, maps and guides in the bar, boars' heads on the walls and great views from the rooms. If you're lucky, José may take you on a tour of his wine cellar to try his 70-year-old *Vino Rancio Aragones* which has a taste not unlike sherry. *Tel 974 48 61 06.*

The road continues sinuously along the ravine, passing Yésero, perched high on the opposite side of the yawning space, and then Gavin. In another 3 km or so you reach Biescas.

Biescas

On the Rio Gallego at the junction of two valleys, Biescas is a useful place to stay in. It's a rather scattered village and not very pretty – in fact its church is positively ugly, more akin to a grain silo than a church – but the surroundings more than make up for the shortcomings.

Casa Ruba
(*hotel,
Biescas*)

Tucked away in a corner just behind the Plaza del Ayuntamiento, in undoubtedly the most attractive part of the village, this is the best placed of Biescas' three hotels, as well as being (marginally) the cheapest. It is comfortable, has a good restaurant and an excellent tapas bar, which is lively with locals much of the day. *Tel 974 48 50 01; closed October and November; price band A.*

⑥ *Leaving Biescas, turn right at the Hotel Giral in the direction of Francia.* The road is excellent from here with several landmarks to watch out for as you progress higher into the Pyrenees. About 4 km after Biescas you pass the Sancturio de Santa Elena (you can visit if you're prepared to drive up a rough, winding track for a couple of kilometres and then walk along a footpath obscured by undergrowth; then you pass the Embalse de Búbal, part of the valley's hydro-electric scheme. An abandoned village beside the lake, Saqués, is presently being restored. ⑦ *Just beyond the lake, turn right for Balneario de Panticosa.*

**Balneario de
Panticosa**
(*detour*)

The drive through the Garganta del Escalar is exciting enough – the road winds up the narrowing, dark gorge beneath meltwater spraying off the rocks. But your arrival at Balneario de Panticosa is no less breathtaking: the turn-of-the century spa village is totally enclosed within a ring of steep, high mountains, the air full of the sound of water gushing down rocky channels. The sulphurous and radioactive qualities of the water springing from the slopes of the Picos del Inferno draw people in search of cures for a variety of ailments. It is also a base for walking, climbing, and in winter, cross-country skiing. The resort also has a casino set in a leafy park and two comfortable three-star hotels, the Gran and Mediodia (despite their barrack-like appearance). Their prices are somewhat high in July and August, but considerably less during the rest of the year.

Return to the main road and turn right in the direction of Francia. Escarrilla comes immediately, a modern village with a choice of places to stay in and not much else, apart from the lovely setting. *In another 6 km, after passing through the Escarra Tunnel, turn right just past the Embalse de Lanuza, one of the more recent additions to the hydro-electric system, into Sallent de Gállego.*

A centre for climbing and fishing, this old village nestling at the foot of the massive Peña Foratata is the most appealing place to stay in between Escarrilla and the border. It has a 15thC church and a Romanesque bridge, beside which is the Hostal Centro, where comfortable rooms are available at a modest price and the restaurant's speciality, of course, is trout. *Tel 974 48 80 19; price band A.*

Back on the pass road you climb steadily, the mountain slopes now more rugged and bare of trees. Just off to the right, El Formigal, a modern ski resort, lively in winter, looks horribly deserted, a real ghost town, at any other time and is best passed by. To the left, the ski slopes don't look their best either, scarred and lined with drag lift pylons. Another 6 km of wild mountain scenery brings you to the frontier.

Up among the high peaks of the Pyrenees, you're almost, but not quite, on top of this part of the world. Straight ahead, across the French border, the distinctive Pic du Midi d'Ossau towers above everything else, while behind, the views extend down the valley towards Sallent. You'll be struck by the difference between the Spanish and French sides. The Spanish side is scattered with numerous duty free and souvenir shops, restaurants and bars; on the French side stands a single hotel, the reasonably priced Casadebaig. If it's a meal you want before driving on, then the hotel's restaurant is by far the most appealing. *Tel 59 05 32 00; closed Oct-May; price band A.*

• *The Dali Museum, Figueres.*

Figueres, on the main road from France to Spain's southern hotspots, seems an unlikely place on which to base a backroads exploration. It does, however, provide access to two of the most interesting regions in this part of Catalunya, the northern Costa Brava and the amazing Garrotxa Natural Park, one of the most important volcanic regions in Europe.

The Costa Brava was unfortunately tarnished by much unfair publicity in the 70s and 80s. Reports focused on unsightly hotel developments and rowdy tourists; but the problems were in fact confined to only one or two small areas in the south; much of the Costa Brava still looks just as natural and wild as it always was. The stretch around Cadaqués and El Port de la Selva, where the influence of the Pyrenees reaches right down to the sea, is a case in point. The scenery and light have also attracted painters for many years and Salvador Dali, who left his considerable mark on the area, was just one of many famous names to live here and draw inspiration from the surroundings. West of Figueres, the Garrotxa is in some ways similar, but in many ways so different. The scenery is just as wild and artists have made their mark here too, especially at Olot. On the other hand, outside of Spain, few people know of it. For backroads explorers, all the more inviting.

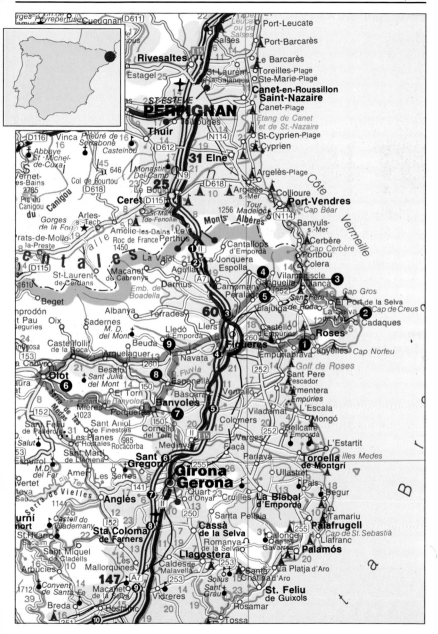

■ **ROUTE ONE: 89 KM**

Figueres

A provincial Catalan town, Figueres would have little to commend it had the surrealist artist Salvador Dalí, who was born there, not decided in the 1970s to open a museum of his works at the town's former theatre.

Crowned with the eggs that became something of a Dalí trademark, the museum was created as a work of art in itself. It may be difficult to understand, but there can be no denying the remarkable quality of his work. Dalí died in 1989 and is buried at the museum.

Just a short walk away is the tree-lined Rambla, the hub of Figueres, with its shops and pavement cafés and two more museums, the Museu de Joguets, specializing in toys, and the Museu de l'Empordà. Just off the Rambla, the Duran is the best town-centre hotel and somewhat cheaper than similar three-star hotels on the outskirts. It also has a first-class restaurant offering a typically Catalan menu. *Tel 972 50 12 50; price band B/C.*

The more modest Hotel Trave is a little farther from the centre on the road to Olot.

From the centre of Figueres follow the signs for Roses. The road passes through one or two uninteresting villages, little more than suburbs of Figueres, and across flat countryside. However in about 8 km you reach Castelló d'Empúries.

Castelló d'Empúries

In the 13thC, the power of the counts of Empúries rivalled that of the counts of Barcelona. Barcelona, however, went on to greater things; Castelló d'Empúries got more or less stuck in time.

Dating from Castelló's 13thC heyday, the Church of Santa Maria is a mixture of Romanesque and Gothic, with an impressive portal and a superb 15thC alabaster retable which, although it pre-dates the great Spanish architect Gaudí by 400 years, is reminiscent of his work.

The former count's palace, with its porticoed courtyard, now serves as the town hall.

Allioli (*hotel/ restaurant, Castelló d'Empúries*)

Disregard this hotel's curious name (*allioli* is garlic mayonnaise) and you'll find a place that is full of rustic charm – the building is a 300-year-old former farmhouse. Just outside the town on the Figueres-Roses road, it makes an extremely attractive and comfortable alternative to staying in the hubbub of Figueres itself. It is also reasonably priced, bearing in mind its three stars. Even if you don't stay here, the restaurant is worth a visit, either for lunch or dinner, but go when you are feeling hungry – the portions are large. The seafood paella is good, as is the Catalan sausage and white beans – a typical local dish. And yes, with every meal you get an *allioli* dip. *Tel 972 25 03 00; closed Dec 17-Jan 18; price band A.*

From the hotel turn right if you want to follow the detour to Roses, and

• *The whitewashed town and beach of Cadaqués.*

follow the signs to Roses, some 10 km. Otherwise continue in the direction of Mas Busca.

Roses
(detour)

In the past, some resorts have given the Costa Brava a bad name, but Roses, originally a Greek fishing village, is not one of them. If you want to sample what this coast can offer, this is one place to start. Despite being the northern Costa Brava's largest resort, it is still quite small, but has long sandy beaches, as well as a large selection of hotels and restaurants.

Return towards Figueres and after 2 km turn right ① at the Hiperjet Hypermercat along a road that takes you through olive groves before winding up into hills sweet with the smell of broom. There are views back to the Bay of Roses and across the plain towards Figueres. Note also the modern windmills. The road winds around Monte Simonets, its summit crowned with radar domes, and then descends to Cadaqués.

Cadaqués

Your second encounter with Salvador Dali: this is where the artist lived for the last 25 years of his life, in a house he built in the 1960s.

The village of white-washed houses, many of them draped in purple bougainvillea, is almost unique on the Costa Brava in conserving its original fishing village atmosphere and avoiding the worst of tourism – helped in this by its unappealing beach. The village, however, is a joy to wander round, with steep, rough cobbled streets leading up to the rather plain church. A view of the church sitting above the little bay features in one of Dali's more down-to-earth paintings. Some of the artist's work can be seen at the Perrott-Moore Museum in the village, while his home is also open to the public.

El Pescador
(restaurant, Cadaqués)

A table by the upper window of this beach-side restaurant gives wonderful views of the bay. Despite the name, there is more on the menu than fish. *Tel 972 25 88 59; price band A.*

Leave Cadaqués the way you arrived. After 5 km ② turn right in the direction of El Port de la Selva. On arriving at the sea front, turn right for the centre.

El Port de la Selva

This is a quiet little resort where fishing still takes precedence over tourism. There are some pleasant sandy beaches and, if you prefer somewhere less developed than Roses, this could be the place for building up the suntan and taking a cooling dip. There are several hotels to choose from, top of the range being the somewhat expensive Porto Cristo *(tel 972 38 70 62)*. The Amberes is more homely, but better value with pleasant views; *tel 972 38 70 30.*

Follow the signs westwards for Llanca and enjoy the views north to Cap Ras. As you approach El Port de Llancà, the wooded hillsides are sprinkled with pink pantiled, whitewashed villas, one of the few modern developments on this otherwise rugged coast. *When you've descended*

• *Monasterio Sant Pere de Rodes.*

more or less to sea-level, turn right into the town.

El Port de Llancà

Standing on an almost enclosed sandy bay, this small resort has grown from nothing over the last 30 years and is popular among the Spanish themselves, who like to stroll along the traffic-free promenade. The sea front here is a haunt of Catalunya's top painter, Martinez Lozano, who sits, complete with artist's beard and smock, at his easel capturing the colourful scene in water colours. There is a choice of restaurants and bars near the harbour.

③ *Leave Llancà in the direction of Figueres and follow the road past the ruins of the Castello de Quermanco, standing on a rocky bluff to the left* ④. *If you want to make the detour described below, take this left turn into*

Vilajuiga, then ⑤ turn left in the village centre, following the signs for Monasterio Sant Pere de Rodes. Drive past broom-covered slopes along a winding road as far as it goes, leave the car in the car park and walk a few hundred metres along a track to the monastery.

Monasterio Sant Pere de Rodes

Built by Benedictine monks in the late 10th and early 11thC, the substantial monastery ruins occupy an outstanding position high on the hill above El Port de la Selva, with sweeping panoramas that extend from Cerbère in France in the north to Cabo de Creus in the east. The nearby chapel of Santa Elena is all that remains of a medieval village that once stood here.

Retrace to Vilajuiga, enjoying different views. If you can drive this part of the route in early evening, you will see the subtle differences in shade between one ridge of mountains and those stacked up behind. *Back in Vilajuiga, turn left, following the* Totes Direcciones *signs, then, through the village, turn first to the right and then shortly left in the direction of Figueres.*

ROUTE TWO: 109 KM

Take the N260 out of Figueres, following the signs for Olot. If you're staying at the Hotel Trave, you'll be well positioned. After 24 km you arrive, via the uninspiring village of Navata, at Besalu.

Besalu

One of the loveliest villages in Catalunya, ancient Besalu, standing at the confluence of the Rios Fluvia and Capellades, is almost totally medieval, though its importance as a strategic and commercial centre goes back even further than that to Roman times. Its Placa de la Llibertat is surrounded by medieval buildings and from the square the Carrer del Pont leads to one of the finest 11thC Romanesque bridges in Spain, complete with cobbles and gateways. It was damaged during the Civil War when two of its arches were blown up, but today this is hardly noticeable. Just into the village from the bridge is sited a *mikwah*, a Jewish ritual bath, one of only three in Europe. If the entrance is locked, you can obtain the key from the tourist office in the Carrer Major, in exchange for your passport.

Curia Reial
restaurant,
Besalu

In a corner of the Placa de la Llibertat, this restaurant and bar occupies a delightful position beside the Fluvia, with a geranium-decked terrace looking down-river to the village's medieval bridge. Even if you're in Besalu at the wrong time for lunch or dinner, you can at least enjoy the view over a drink. If you are here in time for a meal, the *Rap al Pebre Verd* – angler fish in green pepper sauce – is an interesting choice. *Tel 972 59 02 63; closed Mon eve, Tues and Feb; price band B.*
Somewhat cheaper and just outside the medieval quarter is the atmospheric Fonda Siqués, *tel 972 59 01 10; closed Dec 24-Jan 19;*

• Eleventh century bridge at Besalu.

price band A. Both restaurants also have reasonably priced rooms.

Continue on the road for Olot. Shortly you'll notice a difference in the landscape as you travel past tree-covered peaks – small extinct volcanoes, more than 40 in total – in an area known as the Garrotxa.

Castellfollit de la Roca

Your first view of this village, one of the most outstanding of the Garrotxa, is when it appears down the valley poised at the very edge of basalt cliffs, its church occupying the dizziest place of all, right at the end of the promontory and overlooking the Fluvia. The place may at first seem less attractive as you eventually wind up to it, but turn left by the clock tower and follow the backstreets through to the church for a journey back into the Middle Ages.

Leave Castellfollit in the direction of Olot, reached in another 8 km.

Olot

This may also seem disappointing at first sight, but park the car in the Placa Verge del Carme, signposted as you drive into the town, and continue on foot along the Carrer Major. A completely different place unfolds. The town has a large artist community and you'll notice the exceptional number of statues, many of them modern, and small art galleries. The town is famous for its religious imagery, also for the manufacture of *barretinos*, the distinctive red caps worn by Catalans on special occasions. The Carrer Major leads via a fairly insignificant Placa Major to the church and beyond to the tree-lined Passeig d'en Blay, at the top of which is the bullring. One of the town's most impressive buildings is here, the ornately decorated Casa Sola-Morales, built in 1781 in Italian Rococo style. There are also several museums, one of the more interesting being the Museu Casal dels Volcans in the municipal park, which explains the area's volcanic origins.

Follow the Totes Direcciones signs out of Olot, then ⑥ turn left towards Santa Pau. A couple of kilometres out of town there is a handy picnic area and a chance to reduce your already leisurely pace to an even more sedate one by taking a horse and carriage ride through the forest. You are now deep in the heart of the volcanic region with a forest of conical peaks all around. Two kilometres farther on, stop at the car park for the most memorable of the volcanoes, the Volca Santa Margarida, a 45-minute walk away, which has a small chapel inside its crater. Back at the road, continue to Santa Pau.

Santa Pau

You could drive straight through Santa Pau unaware that you were missing anything. It looks most unimpressive from the road, but if you turn off to the right, park in the tiny car park and continue on foot to the centre, you'll walk into a magnificent little medieval gem, a walled village with its Placa Major surrounded by arcaded houses, a church and a castle. Flowers adorn long wooden balconies and there are humourous little sculptures, one particularly life-like of a little girl standing beside a wall, another of a pair of hands cupped to catch water from a tap.

Return to the road and continue towards Banyoles, passing the small villages of El Sallent and Mieres, the latter overlooked by a medieval church and cypress trees. Drive through Porqueres and arrive at Banyoles, where you turn left towards the lake.

Banyoles

A lively and popular holiday town, Banyoles stands beside a lovely lake which for years has been holding major water sports competitions – in 1992 the resort hosted the rowing events of the Barcelona Olympic Games. The inhabitants are sporty, too – witness the numbers walking, jogging or riding bikes along the roads and tracks surrounding the lake. If you don't feel so energetic, you could retire to one of the cafés and watch the action.

Drive clockwise round the lake, and in a couple of kilometres you come to Porqueres' delightful Sant Maria church, the best example of Romanesque architecture in the area. Once you have grown accustomed to the interior gloom, you'll see some quite fine statues.

Return to Banyoles and follow the signs for Girona until reaching a

• *Santa Maria church, Porqueres.*

roundabout with a modern sculpture in the middle. Here follow the signs for Olot and Figueres and then at the edge of the town ⑦ turn right for Figueres. Soon a sign to the left indicates a mirador from where there is a view of the lake. Continue to Esponella.

Esponella

Lying just off the road down a barely discernible narrow lane opposite the Can Roca restaurant, this small village sits in a commanding position above the Rio Fluvia. There is nothing special to see, but wandering through the ancient streets is a step back in time. Even the greenery sprouting from the honey-coloured stone tower of the Romanesque and Gothic church has a certain charm.

Can Roca
(*restaurant, Esponella*)

Situated on the road past the village – you are unlikely to miss it. Good-value Catalan cooking such as tasty charcoal-broiled rabbit or asparagus with ham. *Tel 972 59 70 12; closed Tues; price band A.*
⑧ *Immediately beyond the restaurant take the road bearing left to Crespià and cross the Fluvia by a medieval bridge (view back to Esponella).*

Crespià

Another village in the Esponella mould, Crespià has a strange looking Romanesque church, Santa Eulalia, complete with belfry, tower and a corner turret. The village is known these days mainly for its honey.

⑨ *In about 6 km you reach a T-junction where turn right to return, via Navata, to Figueres.*

The countryside between Burgos and Soria is an almost forgotten part of Spain. Yet this region is known as the 'cradle of Castille': the kingdom which led the Christian reconquest from the 11thC and together with Aragón formed the basis for united Christian Spain. Poor stone villages and solidly built monasteries and churches of that era abound and somehow seem conscious of their formative role in the country's early history.

The cold climate and rough agriculture has bred tough, practical people. Their buildings are simple yet robust, built to stand the test of centuries. The food is straightforward yet full of flavour: ideal for hardworking folks. Roast lamb and roast kid are favourites; also fresh trout from the mountain streams and vegetables cooked with cured ham to give them a rich taste. The wines, typically from Rioja just to the north, are strong in body.

The countryside, particularly to the east of Salas de los Infantes (Route One) is some of the wildest and most varied in Spain. There are fabulous views and a peaceful, timeless feel; it is one of the most unchanged parts of Spain. Wildlife is plentiful: deer, wild boar and partridge all inhabit the forests and oak-covered scrubland, but they are shy and unused to humans, and so difficult to glimpse.

This is not a region for smart restaurants and lavish hotels, except in Covarrubias and Santo Domingo de Silos where the hotels are full of atmosphere and the restaurants typically Castillian.

To the west of Salas de los Infantes (Route Two) the medieval towns of Santo Domingo de Silos and Covarrubias demonstrate the emerging influence of the Kingdom of Castille in the 11th and 12thC. The beauty of the collegiate church in Covarrubias and the exceptional architecture and stonework of the Romanesque cloister in Santo Domingo de Silos highlight the religious motivation and dedication of that period. Nor is the atmosphere purely intellectual. One can take a break to eat just as well as any Count of Castille and in Covarrubias the little shops are a pleasant diversion from a surfeit of religious monuments.

ROUTE ONE: 227 KM (WITH DETOURS)

Salas de los Infantes

The town dates from the 10thC and derives its name from the Castillian legend of a feud which resulted in several children being beheaded. The skulls are said to lie in a tomb in the town's Gothic church. Despite the robust past, Salas is rather uninspiring. Hotal Moreno (*tel 947 380 135*) provides adequate modern accommodation but there are places with more character in other towns nearby. Several shops will provide food for a picnic.

Leave Salas de los Infantes ① on the road signposted Quintanar de la Sierra. Pass through Castrillo de la Reina and Palacios de la Sierra. After 24 km, turn left to Quintanar de le Sierra.

Quintanar de la Sierra

Quintanar prospers from its active sawmills and is also a popular summer base for explorers of the almost uninhabited high sierra to the north. In the town centre, an imposing Ayuntamiento (town hall) faces a spacious tree-lined Plaza Mayor with its incongruous bandstand reminiscent of a seaside resort. Also in the Plaza Mayor stands Hostal Casa Ramón. Don't be put off by the noisy smoke-filled bar: there is a good restaurant on the first floor and clean, unsophisticated accommodation - (*tel 947 395 007; price band B*). Further down the hill from Casa Ramón on the other side of the road, Sr. Mediavilla in the *drogería-ferretería* is a helpful source of local information.

The real attraction of Quintanar lies in its superb setting at the foot of the Sierra de Neila amongst the pine forests which surround it. In the 10thC Quintanar was an important centre in the emerging Kingdom of Castille. About 4 km outside the town, following signs to the Necropolis, are the remains of a Mozarabic cemetery of that era with some most unusual vertical stone tombs.

Laguna Negra de Neila
(detour)

From the centre of Quintanar, ②, follow signs to Laguna Negra (14 km). A twisting bumpy road winds up through the pine forest on to the high open space of the Sierra de Neila. About 2 km before the Laguna Negra there is a spectacular view from the 'Mirador San Franciso'. From here the rivers flow away to the east into the Mediterranean and to the west to the Atlantic.

The Laguna Negra itself lies at an altitude of nearly 2,000 m. It is an attractive spot for a picnic and a quick swim for those who like icy water. It is also popular with fishermen and is stocked with trout from a hatchery in Quintanar.

(From the Laguna Negra it is possible to take a short cut past the village of Neila to Huerta de Arriba. In Huerta de Arriba continue to join the C113, turning left for Salas. This cuts the distance of Route One by about half. Not passable if there is snow.)

To continue on the main route from the Laguna Negra, return to Quintanar, pass through the village, and turn left towards Covaleda.

After 3 km the road passes the Ermita Revenga on the left, the meeting point for an annual pilgrimage of local villages on the last Sunday of May. It is also the site of 9thC tombs similar to those at Quintanar de la Sierra.

Covaleda   A sleepy little village typical of central Castille: you suspect that the daily routine has not changed for years. Perhaps because of its relaxed atmosphere, the village is popular in summer as a base for excursions and walks in the nearby peaks of the Sierra de Urbión. The River Duero rises in these mountains and later flows through the Duero valley providing the life-blood of the Duero wines: less well-known than the Riojas, less heavy in taste, and in the case of the famous Bodega Vega Sicilia, of exceptional quality. Finally, the Duero (called the Douro in Portugal) flows through the heart of the port-producing region of northern Portugal.

Pinares del   A comfortable stop with a restaurant; however it lacks a view of the
Urbión *(hotel,*   countryside and, being newly built, lacks some character. *Tel 975 370*
Covaleda)   *533; price band C.*

From Covaleda continue 11 km to Salduera with its pretty church by the River Duero. In another 1 km the road reaches a junction by a bridge over the Duero. Turn right over the bridge to the little village of Molinos del Duero.

Molinos del   This village was once an important cart-making centre: it has even been
Duero   described as a Detroit of the Middle Ages. Its past prosperity accounts for its smart, substantial houses and general air of superiority over its neighbouring hamlets.

Embalse   *From Molinos,* **(3)***, take the road towards Abejar (away from the bridge we*
(reservoir)   *crossed to reach Molinos). After only about 100 m turn left down a gated*
de la Cuerda   *road.*
del Pozo   For about 3 km this road passes through scrub-covered pasture
and Playa   before disappearing into the reservoir. The final stretch has plenty of
Pita   open spaces with views over the reservoir: ideal for a picnic.
(detour)   *Alternatively, follow the Abejar road for about 5 km before turning left to Playa Pita. Here is a sandy beach on the shores of the reservoir as well as camping facilities, bars and so on. It can be very busy at weekends during the summer, and throughout August.*

Retrace to Molinos, cross the bridge and turn right at the junction, signposted Vinuesa and Laguna Negra (SO 840).

Vinuesa   Vinuesa is a busy village lying on another arm of the Embalse de la Cuerda del Pozo.
It's worth a quick detour for its narrow streets which open on to an

unexpectedly large Plaza Mayor dominated by a 10thC Gothic church. Leading off the Plaza, in the street opposite the church, there are a number of smarter houses with balconied façades typical of the style of the mountain villages of this region.

Continue on the SO 840 and about 1 km out of Vinuesa turn left, ④, following signs for Laguna Negra and Montenegro de Cameros.

Laguna Negra de Urbión

After nearly 8 km, ⑤, turn left, following signs to Laguna Negra. The road twists up through the pine forest; in summer the heather and broom provide striking colour. *After approximately 8 km, on reaching a junction at a sign for a bar, turn left and follow the dirt road to the end where you can park.*

It is a five-minute walk to the laguna, which lies at the foot of a semi-circular rock face rising several hundred feet above the clear, dark water of the glacial lake, fed by ice-cold water from two waterfalls pouring from the cliffs. It is an extraordinarily beautiful scene: perhaps too beautiful for its own good, since large numbers of visitors make their way here in summer.

Retrace about 9 km to the road from Vinuesa and turn left following signs for Montenegro de Cameros.

Puerta de Santa Inés

The road climbs through pine forest, heather and broom to emerge into the open as it passes over Puerta Santa Inés (1,735 m) at the head of the Valle de Revinuesa. This is another superb spot for a picnic with views to the north over the La Rioja area and back to the south over a sea of pine forests. It is also a useful spot to park the car for a walk.

Montenegro de Cameros

Follow the winding road down the valley side to the village at the bottom, with views of this peaceful and pretty valley.

At the foot of the valley lies Montenegro de Cameros with its houses strung out on a steep hillside: another village with an air of peaceful seclusion from events outside the valley. ⑥ *You can follow narrow winding streets up through the village to the church at the top and then past the cemetery to a very sharp left turn to Viniegra. Alternatively, leave the village on the left and follow the road for nearly 1 km. Take the sharp left-hand turn to Viniegra. Shortly, the road from the top of the village joins from the left.*

Continue to Viniegra, climbing through high rolling pasture with wonderful views of the surrounding sierra. After the pass there are a series of tight twisting bends as you drop down to the wooded valley on the other side. The pine forests give way to beeches, oaks and chestnut trees as the road follows the river through rocky gorges past the two Viniegras (de Arriba and de Abajo). This area is a national reserve and rich in wildlife, especially wild boar and deer.

Goyo
(Hotel and restaurant)

Eventually, about 12 km after Viniegra de Arriba, the road meets ⑦ the C113 from Salas de los Infantes to Najera. At this junction is Hostal Goyo. Although unprepossessing, it is a pleasant stop for lunch (1.30 pm to 4.00 pm) and serves several *Riojana* specialities as well as excellent roast lamb and roast kid. It is popular with locals. There is a simple but clean and modern hostal attached as well as more basic accommodation above the restaurant itself. *Tel 941 378 007; price band B.*

From this junction it is 57 km back to Salas de los Infantes on the C113.

For the first stretch the road clings to the side of the reservoir, the Embalse de Mansilla, following every inlet along the pine and beech covered banks before emerging into open pasture. As you approach Salas de los Infantes, the huge ridge line on the other side of the town dominates the skyline and the valley opens out into a wide plain of deep red Rioja soil.

ROUTE TWO: 85 KM

From Salas de los Infantes follow the N 234 for approximately 12 km to ⑧ Hortigüela.

For a detour to Quintanilla de las Viñas continue on the N 234 for another 7 km. Turn right at a sign to the 7thC Ermita. Go through the village following signs for 'information'. On the way through the village, pick up the guide at a house marked Turismo. (This may not be necessary on summer weekends as he spends the day by the Ermita waiting for the next visitor.) At a T junction at the end of the village turn right; after 400 m fork left up to the Ermita.

Quintanilla de las Viñas

The Ermita is in fact a beautifully kept Visigothic chapel remarkable for its age, dating from the 7thC. Only the apse and transept remain, but the scroll work on the exterior walls is most attractive and in excellent condition. Inside the motifs are repeated on the arches. Other reliefs include an exceptional Visigothic Christ and Madonna.

In the grounds the foundations of the original chapel are visible as are some of the stone tombs.

On your way back you could stop at the village bar to absorb the atmosphere of this typical farming community. *Retrace on the road to Hortigüela where you turn right to Covarrubias.* On the left a huge cliff face runs parallel to the road. On a hot day this is a favourite spot for kites and eagles to soar in the currents of rising air.

San Pedro de Arlanza

After 5 km you reach ⑨ the ruined monastery of San Pedro de Arlanza in a wonderfully romantic spot on the banks of the River Arlanza. The monastery, founded in 912, was the burial place of Fernán González, founder of the Kingdom of Castille. Castille played a crucial role in the reconquest of Spain from the Moors and in the 15thC joined with the Kingdom of Aragón to unify the whole of Spain.

Lately, the monastery has fallen into disrepair and its treasures have been distributed to museums in Spain and throughout the world. Nevertheless, the ruins retain their dignity: they seem to be aware of their importance in Spanish history. The little ruined chapel that looks down from a nearby hill marks the spot for all passers-by.

Although the monastery is locked, the curator and restoration staff will sometimes open it for a short guided tour.

Covarrubias Covarrubias was recaptured from the Moors at the end of the 9thC and formed a line of fortified towns on the banks of the Arlanza and Duero rivers. It was the base for the growing influence of the counts of Castille as they established their independence from the Kingdom of Léon.

At weekends it thrives as visitors arrive from Madrid and Burgos to stroll through the town before an enormous lunch of roast lamb or fresh river trout. At weekends, parking can be difficult within the walls of the town: park outside the tall gatehouse which greets you on your arrival from San Pedro de Arlanza and walk the short distance into the Plaza Mayor. The 16C gatehouse was originally an archive for the region of Castille designed by the architect of the Escorial, Juan de Herrera.

Wandering into the Plaza Mayor you see the palace of Fernán González, now much altered from the original building of which only the main door survives. The palace is now the *Ayuntamiento* (Town Hall). Outside the plaza, on the opposite side to the archive, stands an unusual tall tower shaped like a truncated pyramid. This is the Torrejón de Doña Urraca, one of the oldest original buildings in the town. Built in the 10thC, the tower bears the name of Fernán González's grand-daughter.

To the left and through a pretty, shaded plaza of workmen's cottages is the collegiate church which dates from the 15thC. The somewhat austere façade gives no hint of the richness of the church and cloisters within. The church and presbytery contain the tombs of many of the early counts of Castille including those of Fernán González and his wife, Doña Sancha, which were brought from San Pedro de Arlanza in 1841.

One of the other attractions of the church is the 17thC organ which has been maintained in excellent condition and is frequently used for recitals by leading organists. Its wooden organ pipes are said to be the secret of its exceptional tone.

In the cloister you will also see a tomb draped with a Norwegian flag: the resting place of Princess Cristina of Norway who married Alfonso X of Castille in 1238, but died after only a few years of marriage.

Off the cloister lies a museum containing a collection of ecclesiastical robes and cloaks of the 15th and 16thC, in remarkable condition. However, the real jewel of the museum is a 15thC triptych of the Adoration of the Magi which is considered to be a masterpiece of

Flemish art. *Cloister and museum open from 10 to 2 and from 4 to 7.30 on weekends; on weekdays, there are visits at 10.30, 1.30, 4.30, 6 and 7.30 only.*

Covarrubias' narrow streets are full of timbered and stone cottages; several shops sell local craft work: a stroll here is not only a pleasure but a way to work up an appetite.

Arlanza
(hotel, Covarrubias)

Occupying an old stone and timbered building on the Plaza Mayor, the hotel is associated with the Parador chain although not itself a Parador. The restaurant serves traditional Castillian fare and on Saturday evenings (except in July and August) dinner is served in the style of a medieval banquet with roast lamb and other local specialities; *tel 947 403 025; price band C.*

Casa Galín
(restaurant, Covarrubias)

In the Plaza Mayor, opposite the Hotel Arlanza, family-run and friendly with more character than the Hotel Arlanza and a more varied menu; *price band A.* Casa Galín also has accommodation, less comfortable than the Hotel Arlanza; *tel 947 403 015; price band B.*

Rejoin the road on which you arrived in Covarrubias and continue along it for about 200 m, leaving the gatehouse on your left. At a crossroads turn left, following signs to Santo Domingo de Silos (BU 902), and cross the bridge over the River Arlanza.

After about 4 km, there is a view to the left of Retuenta, a little farming village of stone houses and red tiled roofs. The wide variety of herbs, lavender and thyme in the scrubland help to make this an excellent area for honey and you can spot beehives in the fields beside the road.

⑩ *Keep following signs for Santo Domingo de Silos and just before reaching the small town note the turning to the right to the Yecla gorge, described below. For Santo Domingo de Silos itself, keep straight on.*

Santo Domingo de Silos

The town owes its existence and its fame to Santo Domingo who, in 1040, and with the help of the first king of Castille, built what he considered to be his ideal of a monastery on the site of earlier ruins. Of Santo Domingo's original building, the wonderful Romanesque cloister has remained completely intact and is considered the finest in Europe. The stone work and the carving on the capitals of the pillars of the lower cloister are particularly fascinating, the work of three stonemasons whose different styles are noticeable in the detail of the carving and the imagery of mythical beasts, birds, plant life and religious scenes.

Beside the cloister is a museum which contains some interesting items from the monastery's old pharmacy, also manuscripts from the extensive library and the intricate and priceless mozarabic chalice of

• The collegiate church, Covarrubias, dating from the 15th C.

Santo Domingo himself.

A visit to the monastery church is also worthwhile especially if the Benedictine choir is singing Gregorian chants, which they do several times a day.

The monastery was abandoned for much of the 19thC but reinhabited by Benedictine monks from France in 1881. At weekends it is busy with visitors and the monks run a small shop where one can buy recordings of the choir's Gregorian chants. They also sell delicious honey. *Cloister and museum open on weekdays from 10 to 1 and from 4.30 to 8; on weekends from 12.30 to 1 and 4.30 to 6; on various saints' days the monastery is closed altogether.* To check in advance, ring the Hotel Tres Coronas – see below.

Santo Domingo de Silos has always been dominated by the monastery and its religious life and was for centuries a halt on the pilgrims' route to Santiago de Compostela. It was also an important regional town and the base for the district judge who was a representative of the king and held jurisdiction over a hundred or more local towns and villages. In addition, the town had an important apothecary, related to the monastery. The owners of the apothecary lived in one of the seigniorial houses facing on to the plaza which has now been restored as the Hotel Tres Coronas.

Tres Coronas
(hotel, Santo Domingo)

All the solid Castillian character of this traditional mansion has been preserved by its family proprietors. They are welcoming, friendly hosts, knowledgeable about the surrounding region and its history. The restaurant has a varied list of specialities, but roast lamb or kid are particularly delicious here. *Tel 947 380 727; price band C.*

There are several other places to eat in the town and some of the restaurant/bars offer basic accommodation.

Yecla gorge
(detour)

Follow the road back towards Covarrubias. Only a few hundred metres out of Santo Domingo de Silos is the turning to the left to Yecla referred to earlier. Follow signs to Yecla and after about 2.5 km the road passes through a tunnel in the rock. Park either side of it.

The Yecla gorge is a deep but very narrow cleft caused by the stream cutting its way through a seam of soft limestone. Beside the entrance to each end of the tunnel steps lead down to a walkway which runs along the bottom of the gorge for its full length. At the end either return on the walkway or climb the steps to the road and walk back through the tunnel. The circuit takes only ten minutes and provides a contrast to the churches and monasteries which dominate the rest of the day.

Retrace into Santo Domingo de Silos. Follow the road through the town and ⑪ continue for nearly 14 km to Hacinas which lies on the N234. For the first few kilometres the road from Santo Domingo de Silos runs through a wide gorge of orange limestone. The colours are very striking, especially in the evening sun.

Turn left ⑫ for Salas de los Infantes to complete the circuit or take a short detour into Hacinas.

Hacinas

The site of a famous victory by Fernán González (see Covarrubias) over the Moors. The village has a recently restored church with traces of its Romanesque origin and, more remarkable, the trunk of a petrified tree.

• Tympanum of Nuestra Señora de la Peña.

The vast central plateau of Spain is divided into North Meseta and South Meseta by a long range of mountains, the Cordillera Central, which cut diagonally across close to Madrid. This tour explores a small portion of the North Meseta around the lovely city of Segovia, and then, for contrast, climbs into the mountains, which here, as the Sierra de Guadarrama, rise so abruptly from the plain below.

The two loops are very different. The excursion into the Segovian countryside yields far more lasting memories than you may imagine from a landscape so flat and featureless. Prominent amongst those memories will be the ancient mellow stone churches (each with a charming columned atrium); the castles; the storks' nests impossibly perched on every tower, spire or stack in sight; and the great feasts of Castillian roast lamb, the province's much-vaunted speciality. The mountains have less character, but the views are lovely, the air invigorating. These are the lungs of Madrid, and the occupants of that fume-choked city escape here in their thousands at weekends; during the week all is quiet. In winter there is skiing, and conditions on the roads may at times be difficult.

Setting out from Segovia, which makes an excellent base for the tour, Route One can be accomplished in a day; for Route Two with its much slower roads, two days are recommended. Although the distance appears long, you can cut it down by leaving the circuit at Puerto de Navacerrada rather than retracing the access leg back to Segovia. An alternative link between Routes One and Two (except in winter) is by the little mountain road which leads from Navafría, just off the N110, to Lozoya and on to Rascafría.

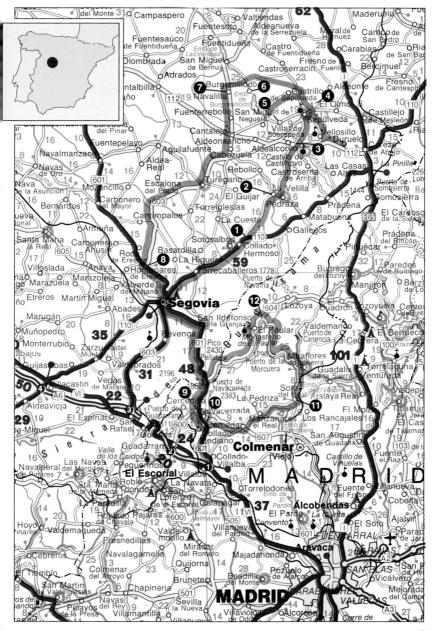

■ **ROUTE ONE: 143 KM**

Segovia

The great aquaduct strides across Plaza Azoguejo, where follow signs to *centro historico*. Parking can usually be found in the streets around San Esteban (street map and sights information available from the tourist office in Plaza Mayor also called Plaza de Franco).

Here is one of the most seductive small cities in Spain, and an ideal centre for the tour. It is graced by three famous monuments: Spain's last Gothic cathedral, the fairytale but fake Alcazar and the 14 km-long Roman aquaduct, in use until just a few years ago. There is also a shower of lovely Romanesque churches, peaceful streets and squares lined by elegant honey-coloured houses. Segovia has a welcome sense of space and an easy-going atmosphere, encapsulated by the gentle evening *paseo* which wends its way along the main thoroughfares. Tourists are easily assimilated, neither solicited nor ignored. Plaza Mayor is the best place from which to start your peregrinations.

Las Sirenas
(hotel, Segovia)

Very well placed, in Calle Juan Bravo, opposite San Martín church. The public areas have an air of matronly dignity, while bedrooms are dull, if perfectly acceptable.

Mesón José María
(restaurant, Segovia)

In Calle Lecea, off Plaza Mayor. Popular and animated, with very good food, including the city's delicious speciality, roast suckling pig. The bar area has the luxury of several tables where you can enjoy your *tapas* or *racionés* – mushrooms in garlic, roast pimientos, *jamón Serrano* and so on – in comfort while the locals stand and chat. Beyond is a large, brightly decorated dining room, equally well patronized by merry Segovian families.

At the roundabout (Plaza Azoguejo) in front of the aquaduct, follow the sign for Soria (N110), and stay on this road. The first village you come to, Torrecaballeros, is plastered with signs proclaiming *horno de asar* (roasting oven); you have entered the land of the Castillian roast suckling lamb and you will not forget it. After Torrecaballeros the geography of your journey becomes plain to see: to the south the black bulk of the Sierra de Guadarrama; to the north the seemingly empty *meseta* which you are about to penetrate.

Sotosalbos

It's worth turning off the road into this scrappy, down-at-heel village to see the lovely Segovian Romanesque church, though not to worry if time is short, for there are more examples to come.

Molino de Río Viejo
(hotel, Sotosalbos)

Entrance on right just past Río Viejo sign between Sotosalbos and Collado Hermoso. Tiny converted mill with only six bedrooms and a communal dining table where basic country fare is served. Rustic and simple in the extreme, yet furnished with flair by its sophisticated owners. Riding can be arranged. *Booking essential; closed when no-one is booked in. Tel 911 403063.*

① *Turn left signposted Sepúlveda and Pedraza. In 10.5 km, at La Vellila, bear right signposted Pedraza.*

Pedraza de la Sierra

Compared to the crumbling villages that are typical of this region, Pedraza comes as a surprise, and a certain sense of unreality hangs in the air. A careful combination of preservation and restoration, it is an immaculate and very pretty medieval village whose massive encircling walls are pierced by just one entrance, the Puerta de la Villa. The irregular shaped Plaza Mayor has upper storey balconies supported by an assortment of stone pillars, and the narrow streets are lined by fine, honey-coloured houses embellished with stout wooden doors and escutcheons. Pedraza's castle guards the village from a rocky promontary with views to the pastoral little valley of the Vellila down below. Its tower was restored and inhabited by the painter Zuloaga (whose work you may have admired in the Casón de Buen Retiro in Madrid); it now houses a small Zuloaga museum. During the week Pedraza feels almost empty, quiet as the grave, its clutch of chi-chi restaurants opening irregularly. At weekends, the place seethes with Madrileños, and the *hornos de asar* roar into life.

La Posada de Don Mariano
(hotel, Pedraza)

Outside the busy periods, you can choose which bedroom you prefer – attic ones are the most charming, but all are attractive and individually decorated with the sophisticated Madrileño in mind. Family-run and worth the highish prices. *Tel 911 509886; booking essential for weekends.*

Pintor Zuloaga
(restaurant, Pedraza)

Well known for its serious Castillian cooking, this is a grand little restaurant with prices to match. The setting is a charming señorial house decorated in traditional Castillian style. There are several restaurants to choose from in Pedraza, but this is reckoned to be the best; part of the Parador chain. *Tel (911)509835; price bands B/C.*

② *At the main road, turn right for Sepúlveda. Leaving fine views of Pedraza behind you, strike out across the stony, red-earth plain.*

Castillo Castilnovo
(detour)

③ *At the crossroads, turn right signposted Cerezo de Abajo. The castle immediately comes into view. Drive off the main road, signposted Castroserna, for a closer view, possibly a picnic stop (do not be tempted to take the car down the pretty Castroserna road, which runs alongside a wooded stream – it has few turning points).* Castilnovo, with its arresting stripes of brick and stone, stands in a pleasant grove. Once a splendid Moorish stronghold, it is now tamed into 20thC domesticity, complete with swimming pool. *Retrace to the main road.*

• *Plaza Mayor,
Sepúlveda.*

Sepúlveda   You should be able to park in the Plaza Mayor. A delightful place to while away a few hours, especially over lunch time, which is from 1.30 pm. The town is distinguished by its crop of Romanesque churches, and by its past as a centre of power and influence. A natural fortress, built on a bluff above the wild and deep Duratón gorge at its confluence with the Río Caslilla, Sepúlveda was buffeted back and forth between Moors and Christians, until empowered and stabilized by the granting of a royal charter *(fuero)* after the Christian reconquest. In the pretty side streets fine houses adorned with coats of arms bear witness to its former glory, and a sense of pride still pervades.

Of the 15 parish churches that existed in the Middle Ages, just a handful remain, all examples of Sepúlvedan Romanesque, which was a precurser of the more refined Segovian Romanesque. At the top of a long flight of steps is the 1,000-year-old El Salvador, with a crudely but

• *Romanesque church at Duratón, with storks' nest on the tower.*

vigorously carved atrium and affectingly simple interior.

Walk away from the town on the road to the right of the castle to see La Virgen de la Peña on a promontory overlooking the gorges. Then return and cross Plaza Mayor to the charmingly simple San Bartolomé.

You have now reached a key point on the Castillian roast lamb trail. Sepúlveda styles itself *Capital Mundial del Cordero Asado*. Where to try the thing? Hernanz *(at the bottom of the steps to El Salvador; also 12 rooms; tel 911 540378)* is highly recommended, but for a basic *figón* (meat only tavern) try Zute El Mayor, known to all as Tinín, below.

Tinín
(restaurant, Sepúlveda)

The room is straightforward, the menu even more so – *cordero asado* so tender that it is parted from the bone with a spoon; a salad, a jug of wine, followed by *tarta ponche* (delicious local cake), *carne de membrillo* (quince jelly served with *manchego* cheese) and a wicked yellow liqueur called El Afilador. The eponymous Tinín officiates with gusto. He will bustle you out to see the roaring furnace in which your hunk of lamb is cooking, and he will proudly tell you that King Juan Carlos has been his guest.

Duratón
(detour)

Leave Plaza Mayor by the road opposite the castle; where the road forks bear left for Duratón, downhill, through rocky terrain. Turn left through the village, signposted Iglesía Románica, and left again over a little bridge.

This typical Segovian Romanesque church is hard to beat for its isolated setting, its lovely atrium complete with delicately carved capitals showing a variety of animals and kings on horseback, and its terrific storks' nest set at a rakish angle. *Return to Sepúlveda.*

④ *Leave Plaza Mayor by facing the castle and taking the Burgos road on the right. Outside the village, turn left signposted Sacramenia and Urueñas. In about 5 km turn left again, signposted Castrillo and Ermita de San Frutos.*

Ermita de   ⑤ *Drive through Castrillo and turn left signposted Cantalejo and Ermita de*
San Frutos   *San Frutos. Goodness, there is the Sierra de Guadarrama again. Park at*
(detour)   *Villaseca.* Having made up your mind about the merits and defects of roast lamb Castillian-style, the ideal way to walk off the after-effects is to take the 5-km track to the little Romanesque chapel of San Frutos, set in spectacular isolation above a loop in the dammed Duratón. Benedictines lived here from 1076 to 1836, but it was a site of worship even before then. *Return to Castrillo, where turn left.*

Castrillo-   As you continue, flocks of sheep, each tended by a shepherd, become
Navalilla   a familiar sight along this stretch. They feed off the herb grass which gives Castillian lamb its flavour. Just beyond Aldehuela de Sepúlveda is one of those Romanesque buildings which pepper the Segovian countryside – a little church (with later bell tower) standing alone among fields, surrounded by lilac blossom in spring: a lovely spot for lazing in the sunshine, listening to nothing more stressful than cicadas and birdsong. The road then winds through a green valley and out into a wild, deserted landscape.

⑥ *At the T-junction, turn left. At Burgomillodo follow the road round to the right, keeping the dam on your left. Here is a completely different landscape of sand and pine.*

⑦ *Turn left at the T-junction beyond Navalilla, signposted Segovia.* The C603 is a fast, little-used road which passes glades of pine around the lush valley of the Cega, and, towards Turégano, huge wheatfields typical of the north *meseta.*

Turégano   Ahead on the dead straight road, the impressive bulk of Turégano's pink-hued castle comes into view, standing in a sea of wheat with the Sierra de Guadarrama as a dark back-drop. The bell tower you can see inside the mainly 15thC castle is a Baroque addition to the lovely Romanesque church of San Miguel which it enfolds. *Open only on request; tel 991 500667.*

The road passes straight through the middle of Turégano's galleried Plaza Mayor, and then on through pleasant countryside. ⑧ *At the CL601 turn left.* First Segovia's vast cathedral, and then its Alcazar, come magnificently into view, heralding the end of this loop.

▰ ROUTE TWO: 142 KM

Leave Segovia by the Madrid road and pick up signs for Puerto de Navacerrada (CL601).

La Granja de San Ildefonso   The attraction here is the garden of La Granja's palace, especially if you are lucky enough to arrive on one of the very infrequent days when the fabulous fountains are playing. (Work is in progress to rectify the problem by boosting the water pressure.) La Granja was built as an austere retreat by Felipe V, first of Spain's Bourbon kings; it was his Italian widow who gave both palace and gardens the Versailles-inspired flourish we see today. The palace, much damaged by fire in 1918, is distinguished by its vast chandeliers from the town's illustrious glassworks, and by the Rococo opulence of its symmetrical state rooms *(open daily)*. The orderly streets of the little town grew up with the express purpose of serving the palace.

Roma *(hotel/ restaurant, La Granja)*   Simple but pleasant *hostal* set conveniently beside the palace gates with a reputable restaurant. *Tel (911)470752; closed Nov to mid-Dec; price band B.*

La Granja-Navacerrada   The road climbs through pine forest to Puerto de Navacerrada at 1,860 m, an ugly accretion of modern chalets and apartment blocks set on a bald mountain top – of interest only if you want to ski there. Descending, first a reservoir comes into view, and then the vast, overbearing crucifix which marks Franco's Civil War memorial, Valle de los Caídos. ⑨ *Just before Navacerrada, at a major road intersection, take the road signposted Colmenar.* To visit the little summer and winter resort itself, you must turn off the main road – perhaps to stock up for a picnic to eat in La Pedriza (see below).

⑩ *At the crossroads (right hand turn signposted to Becerril), make a difficult sharp left-hand turn signposted Mataelpino. Just before Mataelpino look out for a sharp turning to the right indicated by a tourist route sign to Manzanares el Real. After Boalo, turn left on to the M608, following signs for Manzanares.*

La Pedriza *(detour)*   With Manzanares castle in sight, shortly after a picnic/barbecue area on the right, turn left signposted La Pedriza Parque Nacional. Part of the southern slopes of the Sierra de Guadarrama, this is a rocky and mountainous region, particularly beautiful in spring when white cistus and blue iris clothe the hillsides. As you drive up the little winding road, holm oak, pine and juniper give way to a spectacular barren landscape of strangely-shaped giant boulders and rushing streams. The information centre at the park's entrance has details of walking and mountaineering. La Pedriza makes an ideal place to picnic, and although popular, especially at weekends, you can always get away by walking a little further from the road than everyone else.

Castillo de Manzanares el Real

Although the setting disappoints, this is a classic square-plan castle, with pleasingly curvaceous corners, bristling with turrets and battlements. It may look warlike, but its life has been entirely peaceful, for it was built by a medieval court poet, the Marquis of Santilana, and converted into a palace by his son. Architect Juan Gras later built the lovely south side *loggia*, added false machicolations, and studded the towers with stone cannon balls *(open daily)*.

⑪ *At Soto del Real turn left signposted Miraflores.*

Miraflores de la Sierra

A pleasant mountain village, lively at weekends, when you are likely to find music and dancing in the plaza. (The opening times of up-market shops – boutique, furniture and so on – bear witness to the hold that Madrileños have over places like Miraflores: they are kept tight shut Monday to Friday.) There are terrific views of La Pedriza from up here. Energetic passengers in your car can walk from Miraflores to the next stop: a five-hour hike leads through the mountains to El Paular.

Las Llaves
(restaurant, Miraflores)

Away from Segovia and Sepúlveda, you will find restaurants offering regional specialities other than *cordero asado.* On Las Llaves' menu are succulent fat white beans, *judiones de La Granja*; *sopa Castellana*; and *cocido*, a stew of chick peas, meat and vegetables, with its broth served first as a soup. *Tel 91 8444057; booking essential at weekends; closed mid-Sep to mid-Oct; price band B.* If the well-regarded Las Llaves is full, you will eat perfectly well in the *comidor* behind the Bar Victoria next door.

From Miraflores a pretty road snakes north into the heart of the Sierra, over the Puerto de la Morcuera and down to the high valley of the Río Lozoya where the sleepy town of Rascafría stands amongst pine and beech.

Los Calizos
(hotel/ restaurant, Rascafría)

Shortly before Rascafría, this restaurant in a peaceful setting has 12 simple and inexpensive rooms, useful for those not planning to spend the night at El Paular. In sunny weather you can eat in the shady garden. *Price band A/B*

⑫ *In Rascafría, turn left for El Paular.*

El Paular

Locked deep in the mountains, the monastery of El Paular is the Sierra de Guadarrama's star prize: a contented though somewhat bizarre marriage of religious tranquillity and four-star luxury. The monastery was founded in 1390 by King Juan I for a community of Carthusian monks and flourished under royal patronage; but by the 19thC the place had fallen into disrepair, the monks gone. Now they are back, this time Benedictine, and El Paular has a new lease of life, both as a monastery and as an expensive hotel (see below). The church holds a delightful surprise, not to be missed: a wonderfully graceful Gothic retable in painted alabaster, highly unusual. The overwrought Baroque screen – the transparente – and the chapel behind the altar – are somewhat cloying, but the cloisters are charming.

Santa María de El Paular *(hotel/ restaurant, El Paular)* Occupying the old cloisters, part of the monastic complex, this pricey hotel sees a very different lifestyle to the one which goes on in the monks' quarters, right next door. The mock-historical decoration hardly does justice to the setting, and the bedrooms are surprisingly sober, even stern, but otherwise all the luxury trappings are here including tennis, swimming and two restaurants. *Tel 91 869 10 1 1; price band B/C.*

The road continues along the Lozoya valley, then ascends to the Puerto de los Cotos through bracing hiking and skiing country. From Valcotos, lifts can take you up to the lagoons below the Pico de Peñalara, the Sierra's highest peak. To complete the route, carry onwards and upwards to the highest pass, Puerto de Navacerrada. For Segovia, turn right; for the A6 motorway turn left.

Our usual figure-of-eight format is not ideal for this magnificent elongated mountain range close to Madrid. We have therefore suggested a linear route which not only suits the terrain, but is worth doing for its own sake; it is also an interesting way to travel from the Madrid area to Portugal (or vice-versa).

You need at least two days to make the most of the scenery. Although this is a popular summer retreat for Spaniards from the nearby Castillian cities, out of season the roads are uncrowded and the mountains are big enough for everyone.

The route begins and ends with grandiose man-made monuments: the Monasterio de El Escorial and the cathedral of Plasencia. In between, nature reigns supreme. There is a striking climatic contrast

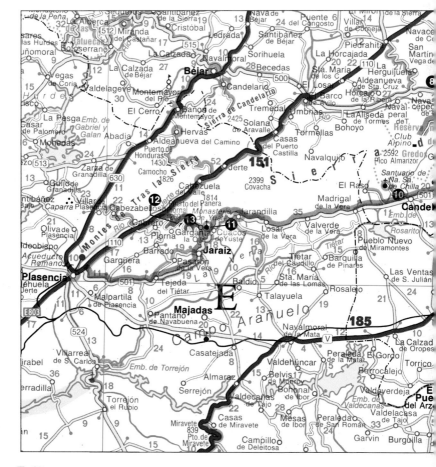

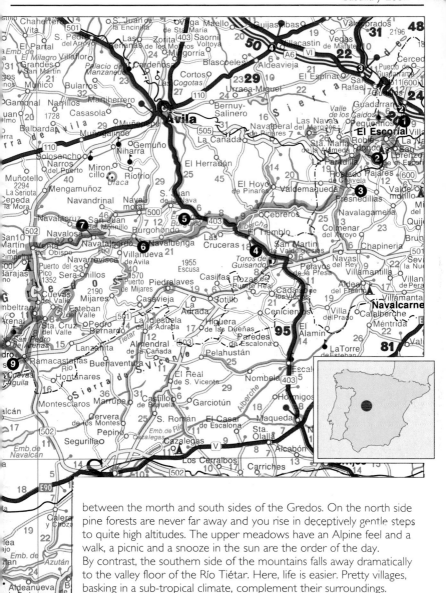

between the morth and south sides of the Gredos. On the north side pine forests are never far away and you rise in deceptively gentle steps to quite high altitudes. The upper meadows have an Alpine feel and a walk, a picnic and a snooze in the sun are the order of the day.

By contrast, the southern side of the mountains falls away dramatically to the valley floor of the Río Tiétar. Here, life is easier. Pretty villages, basking in a sub-tropical climate, complement their surroundings. Flowers fill the balconies and produce hangs to dry in the sun; orange blossom scent hangs in the air.

ROUTE: 248 KM

San Lorenzo de El Escorial

Pious Felipe II commissioned the Monasterio de El Escorial, partly in response to his father Carlos V's command to build a royal mausoleum, and partly as a dedication to St Lawrence, whose church Spanish troops had destroyed when capturing the French town of St Quentin in 1557. The resulting monastery-cum-palace-cum-mausoleum was built between 1563 and 1584. It is vast, and visiting it is a daunting experience. The forbidding exterior is best seen in bright sunshine, or softly lit after dark. Inside there is an oppressive display of royal and not-so-royal tombs in the mausoleum. On the guided tour you will see endless famous paintings and other art treasures; Felipe's stark rooms, as well as the more opulent quarters of the later Bourbons; even then you will only scratch the surface. It is worth hunting out the magnificent library, cleverly designed to preserve the priceless books and manuscripts. There is also an interesting exhibition in the Palace basement, giving details of the men and machinery behind El Escorial's construction.

Parilla Príncipe
(hotel, Escorial)

This fashionable town heaves with escaping Madrileños at weekends and is best visited midweek. The same applies to this elegant and sophisticated restaurant, close to El Escorial with small but comfortable rooms at reasonable prices. *Floridablanca 6; tel 91 8901611.*

La Cueva
(restaurant, Escorial)

A lively tapas bar and restaurant concealed within a warren of rooms set on three floors around a galleried and painted entrance hall. *San Anton 4; tel 91 8901516; price band B.*

Silla de Felipe II
(detour)

Take the Avila road and ①, turn left past the golf course. Seats are hewn out of the rock and Felipe II is supposed to have watched the building of El Escorial from this superb vantage point.

San Lorenzo de El Escorial - El Tiemblo

Return to the M505 and continue in the direction of Avila. ② carry straight on at the crossroads where the road becomes the M534. This enchanting drive through beautiful umbrella pine forests is the perfect pastoral antidote to the austerity of El Escorial.*③ Turn right after Robledo de Chavela.* Donkeys laden with panniers may be your only companions on this rural route which passes through Cebreros, famous for its wine, and continues to El Tiemblo.

El Tiemblo

Set somewhat unattractively alongside the N403, it is nonetheless a useful stop if you want to buy picnic ingredients. Head for the shops in the village centre, to the west of the main road, and if you should stumble across the quaint Baroque church, so much the better.

Toros de Guisando
(detour)

Head towards San Martín de Valdeiglesias and ④, turn right where

• *Rio Alberche, Sierra de Gredos*

signposted to Arenas de San Pedro and Toros de Guisando. Four Celtic Iron-Age animals stand in a row, as if in some ancient children's playground, surrounded by peaceful fields. They are easily missed as they are hidden from the road by a wall, on which is a plaque marking the place where, in 1468, Henry IV proclaimed that his sister Isabel should be Queen of León and Castille after his death. The Iron-Age creatures, more pig than bull, are confusingly named since they are not near Guisando, but found singly throughout this area. They are thought to have marked the boundaries of the various Celtic tribes. Whatever their true meaning they are a curiously uplifting sight.

Alberche Valley

Return to El Tiemblo, and continue past it on the N403. ⑤ Turn left for Navaluenga and Burgohondo on the AV902, 12 km from El Tiemblo. The road leads down to the far end of the Embalse de Burguillo, (one of many half-filled reservoirs) which sits unnaturally at the entrance to the hidden valley of Río Alberche. To see this river, (which is a fisherman's paradise), park where the fence ends and stroll down amongst the pines to the edge of the fast-flowing water where wild mint grows amonst the boulders.

Navaluenga -
Venta
del Obispo
The road soon leaves the river, passing through flat, open countryside. ⑥ *At the T-junction in Burgohondo, (where there is a pony trekking centre, El Madroño, tel 91 283191), turn left on the AV901 and up the hill turn right on to the AV903.* The road starts to climb towards the peaks of the Gredos. Initially the land is divided into small vineyards by a maze of stone walls and the hillside is covered in pale cream broom in May. ⑦ *At the T-junction (the highest point of this road) turn left on to the C500 to Navatalgordo.* The villages here are messy, unfinished affairs, as if they have given up any hope of competing with the magnificent landscape. The road, while steep and winding, is well surfaced and quiet. The harsh countryside is punctuated by streams and these feed lush patches of grass where animals graze contentedly. Roofed stone shelters dot the hillside, almost indistinguishable from their surroundings. Once through the strange village of Navalosa where the old stone houses have been abandoned in favour of an ugly modern sprawl, Pico Almanzor, snow capped until early June, the highest peak in the Gredos, looms to the left.

Parador de
Gredos
(hotel,
Gredos)
In Venta del Obispo turn left in the direction of Arenas de San Pedro and then right on to the C500 for Parador de Gredos. The first Parador to be opened (1920s) was built on this specially selected site, 1,580m high with unrivalled views of the mountains. The interior is designed to resemble a hunting lodge with large reception rooms, comfortable and spacious bedrooms and generously equipped bathrooms. It is a just reward for the tortuous journey and very good value. The large sunny dining room has picture windows overlooking the pine forests and the food is good if somewhat anonymous. An excellent centre for exploring the north side of the Gredos with information on riding, walking, climbing, and in winter, skiing. *Tel 920 348048.*

Pico
Almanzor
(detour)
Head towards El Barco de Avila and ⑧, turn left just before Hoyos del Espino on the AV931. The road pierces the heart of the Gredos: it passes over a gentle river, the early stages of the Río Tormes – a fine picnic place. Continue on to El Plataforma, the car park at the end of this road. From here you can follow the well-marked two-hour walk known as the Circo de Laguna Grande. On summer weekends it can become a rather depressing shuffle when the huge lake is a favourite picnic site but at all other times it is a glorious walk. It is possible to extend the route, climbing over the top of the Gredos and descending to Candeleda, thus experiencing the extraordinary change in terrain at first hand. Wildlife includes the now-protected ibex and wheeling birds of prey.

Puerto del Pico

Rejoin the N502 for Arenas de San Pedro. A fast, well-maintained road takes you over this pass from which you can see the southern slopes of the Gredos fall breathtakingly to the valley below. You'll also see a well restored Roman road snaking up the mountain. The valley is intensely cultivated with terraces of olives, fig trees, citrus trees and your first glimpse of palms.

Mombeltrán

This 14thC castle belonging to the Dukes of Albuquerque, with its fat round towers at each corner, is just as you imagine a Spanish castle should be, and is perfectly situated on a grassy hummock just below the village, surrounded by olive trees. *Turn left in the village and park in the small square alongside the castle.* View the castle while drinking a coffee in one of the cafés: close up, the barbed wire and a general air of neglect spoil the magic. The 15thC Gothic church, with its incongruously grand stairs to the choir is worth looking at before carrying on down to the valley floor.

Cuevas del Aguila
(detour)

⑨ *Follow signs to Ramacastañas and at the T-junction in the village turn left and then immediately right to the caves, along a bumpy road in need of repair.* Standing amongst the trees that surround the caves the mountains look almost unreal – like a painted backdrop. Inside, the natural formations of stalactites and stalagmites have been cleverly and sympathetically lit to form fantastic shapes such as the Three Wise Men bringing gifts to the Virgin Mary, as well as more mundane objects including a tortoise and a cauliflower. You many need to use your imagination to determine the objects as guided tours are only in Spanish. *Open all year, 10.30-6.*

Arenas de San Pedro

This is the commercial centre of the Gredos and despite its Roman bridge and ruined castle it is not very appealing. There is a tourist information office. You can strike out from Arenas for the mountain villages of El Arenal, El Hornillo and Guisando, base camps for serious walkers. Guisando, which is renowned for its rock climbing school, is picturesque but perhaps not worth another gear wrenching climb when there are lovelier villages to come in the valley.

Hostería Los Galayos
(restaurant/ hotel, Arenas)

Despite its garish bar, the rooms are comfortable and modern. The cellar restaurant, *El Bodegón*, had some character and specializes in the traditional *asador* (spit-roast). *Plaza del Castillo 2; tel 918 371379; price band B.*

Candeleda

The valley widens as you approach the village and you enter through an avenue of palm trees, into streets lined with orange trees. The oldest part of the town is to the left, with narrow streets and the ubiquitous projecting wooden balconies.

Mesón Pedros
(restaurant, Cendeleda)

⑩ *Turn left for the old town at the roundabout (signposted Oropesa),* and en route for the old town have lunch with the locals at Mesón Pedros. Cheery red tablecloths, friendly service and hearty regional food. *Ramon y Cajal 3 & 6; tel 918 380839; price band A.*

Valley of La Vera

Before entering Extremadura, you pass the turning to Castro de El Raso – site of a Celtic Iron-Age hillside fort, which has been extensively excavated. Once in the vicinity of La Vera – a fertile shelf above the Rió Tiétar – the sub-tropical vegetation continues, watered by *gargantas* – chutes of melted snow that course down the mountains. Don't be put off by what you see of the villages from the main road. To view their hidden charms you must park your car, and follow the signs, on foot, to the *centro urbano.* Villanueva de la Verde has an enchanting arcaded *Plaza* with a central fountain. Tiny streets with charming little houses radiate off it and there is a mass of flowers on every balcony. In Valverde de la Vera the narrow cobbled streets have central channels running with water. Losar de la Vera's claim to fame lies in its topiary. Geometrical shapes and animals line the main road, cleverly diverting your attention from the nondescript modern buildings.

Parador Carlos V
(hotel, Jarandilla)

This converted 14thC castle was home to gouty Emperor Carlos V while he waited for his final retirement home to be completed at Yuste. A Renaissance gallery overlooks a cool inner courtyard and there is a swimming pool among the rose gardens. The bedrooms are as well equipped as you would expect from a hotel of this class. Only the soulless bar is out of place.

Cuacos

The 16thC houses of the Plaza Mayor attract more visitors than those in other villages along the route, possibly because Don Juan, Carlos V's illegitimate son, stayed in one of them when visiting his father.

Monasterio de Yuste
(detour)

⑪ *Turn sharp right when entering Cuacos.* Crippled by gout, Carlos V had to be carried in a litter to end his days in this idyllic woodland retreat. Four simple rooms were added to an existing Jeronymite monastery. His bedroom was designed so that he could watch mass being celebrated in the church next door, even when bedridden. This idea was copied by his son Felipe II at El Escorial, but in every other respect there cannot be two more different palaces. The gardens around the pond where the Emperor bathed while seated stiffly on his horse are tended by the closed order of monks. The air in May is perfumed with philadelphus and without hordes of visitor the place is magical.

Garganta la Olla
(detour)

You can continue from Yuste along a simple but surfaced mountain road to this lively village. There are plenty of little bars dotted about its curious narrow streets. It is not a tourist village and visitors are a cause for curiosity. The butcher's shop is painted blue, denoting its previous existence as a brothel for the soldiers of Carlos V. ⑫ *For a truly dramatic but strictly fair weather route over the mountains, carry on over the Puerto del Piornal to the Jerte valley.*

For a less adventurous, but also attractive route, return to Cuacos and go directly to Plasencia on the C501.

For some last-minute rural relaxation before reaching the city of Plasencia, ⑬ turn right just outside Cuacos at the large sign to El Largo. The road takes you to the Garganta de Pedro Chate, where an artificial lagoon has been formed: perfect for swimming. There is a shady café for snacks and drinks by the river and you can walk up through the trees alongside the *garganta. Carry on the way you are going to get back to the main road.*

Plasencia   The heart of Plasencia is the traffic-free Plaza Mayor. On Tuesday mornings it has a wonderful fruit and vegetable market – all the more mouthwatering after the vegetable-free Castillian diet. Busy bars and shops radiate off the *plaza* where local farmers meet to discuss life. What Plasencia lacks in good looks it makes up for in hustle and bustle, and the lack of concessions to tourism is refreshing. The cathedral (Iglesia de Santa Maria) is something of a jumble: it consists of the old Romanesque cathedral (now a museum) and the new (16thC) Gothic cathedral. The original idea was for the latter to replace the original but money ran out and we are left with the two buildings rather awkwardly joined together. Surrounded by imposing mansions, the cathedral and its surroundings are the pleasantest part of the city.

Mi Casa   This large restaurant is popular enough for its size not to be
(restaurant/   intimidating, and the central location makes it a convenient place to
hotel,   stay in. *Maldonado 13, (also called Calle Patalón); tel 927 411450; price*
Plasencia)   band A.

Alfonso VIII   Definitely the smartest place in town, with prices to match. Patronised
(hotel,   by businessmen with expense accounts, it is on the main road. *Calle*
Plasencia)   *Alfonso VIII 34; tel 927 410250; price band C.*

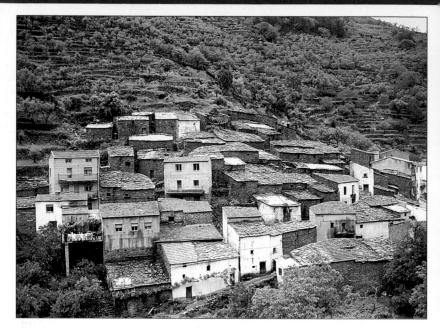

*• El Gasco,
deep in Las
Hurdes.*

Out west, beyond the university city of Salamanca, there lies
a region of cattle country and mountain, peppered with
towns which are far more isolated and, in their way, as beautiful
as Salamanca. For some, the cattle country is truly addictive, with
wide-spaced carob trees and holm oaks throwing down little
pools of shade on a swelling countryside that is as green and
flowery as a brocade in spring and as tawny as a lion's pelt by
end of summer. Black cattle and pigs – the famous *pata negra*
breed or 'blackfoot' from which the best of Spanish hams derive
– inhabit this wild if curiously park-like countryside. But hot it
certainly can be; then the mountains, always a few degrees
cooler, exert a compulsive pull. They lie along the southern
borders of the province of Salamanca, in Castilla y León, and
they range down into Cáceres in the region of Extremadura, a
part of Spain even further from the beaten track.

The route begins and ends in Ciudad Rodrigo, Roderick's
City, one of the loveliest and quirkiest in Spain, crosses a tract of
cattle country and dallies in two different mountain ranges, both
marked by their own delightful vernacular architecture. This is
genuine backroads driving-fill up with petrol before you start.

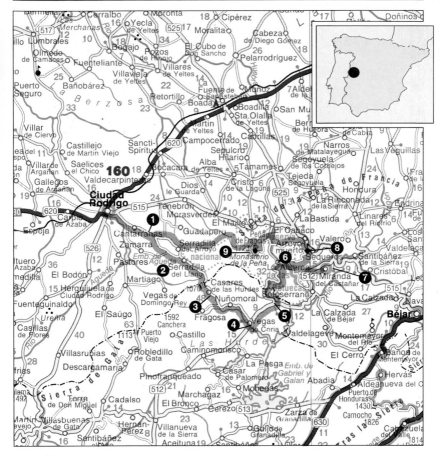

ROUTE: 170 KM, WITH A 40-KM DETOUR

Ciudad Rodrigo

Count Rodrigo González Girón gets the credit for founding the original city in 1150, but it was the king of Castile himself, later in the 12thC, who ordered up the walls that still surround it. These remain magnificently in place, trimmed in height during later centuries and reinforced with ditches and star-pointed outer bastions. In the Napoleonic Wars, they first held out the French in a cruel siege and later, when Ciudad Rodrigo had capitulated, allowed the French to hold it temporarily against the British under the Duke of Wellington. This second siege lasted 11 bitter days before Wellington overran the city, leaving the cathedral well pocked by cannonballs. Wellington became the Duke of Ciudad Rodrigo,

• *Plaza Mayor,
Ciudad Rodrigo.*

a courtesy title still held by the family.

You can walk right round the walls in the cool of evening, admiring the sun as it descends over Portugal. Within the walls, there is a tremendous collection of fine houses and handsome late medieval alleys, enough escutcheons to fill a dozen furniture lorries, barley sugar columns, richly carved windows. The much-admired Gothic cathedral has some of the most profusely carved, and often amusing, cloister capitals in Spain; the post office occupies a mansion with a Mudéjar interior and Renaissance wrought-iron grilles while the Plaza Mayor has a triumphantly beautiful town hall, its sweeping balconies rising over equally graceful ground-floor arcades.

At carnival time the Plaza Mayor is the scene of a thrilling *encierro* or running and stockading of the bulls.

El Sanatorio
*(bar/
restaurant,
Ciudad
Rodrigo)*

El Sanatorio is a bar and modest eatery – fried belly of pork and a suitably rough red wine. It is also a temple to the *encierro*, its walls crammed with ancient photographs of horsemen bringing in the bulls through open countryside and then, once in the city, the spills and drama of amateur bullfighting in the Plaza. *Plaza Mayor 12; tel 923 46 00 24; price band A.*

**Parador de
Ciudad
Rodrigo**
*(hotel, Ciudad
Rodrigo)*

The Castle of Enrique 11 of Trastámara occupies the only stretch of the town wall that cannot be walked. The ivy-grown castle is itself largely occupied by the parador. Some rooms have very limited views, but the atmosphere is pleasant and the splendid dining room offers a good local (as well as a Spanish/international) menu. *Plaza del Castillo 1; tel 923 46 01 50; restaurant price band B/C.*

Leave Ciudad Rodrigo to the south-east on the minor road signposted Serradilla del Arroyo and La Atalaya, with the Ambulatorio de la Seguridad Social building on your left. Keeping left shortly at Sanjuanejo, you will soon run into a thrilling terrain of holm oak and acebuche or wild olive, with pata negra pigs trotting or snoozing beneath and red kites circling watchfully above.

After nearly 13 km, ① keep right for Serradilla del Llano, declining the left-hand option for Serradilla del Arroyo.

Climbing now through hillsides rich in cistus, wild lavender and broom, you will reach Serradilla del Llano, about 22 km from Ciudad Rodrigo. It's a scrap of a place ushering in sweeping views of valley and up beyond to the long ridges of the Sierra de la Canchera, dividing line between Salamanca and Cáceres. Now the road runs up into the mountains, heather giving way to pines and with some damage from forest fire – a special curse in this part of Spain – to cross the border and drop at once into a dramatically altered terrain. Now the valleys are precipitous and tight, with fruit trees growing on narrow terraces and views of villages below with dark slate roofs. This is Las Hurdes, once the most isolated and still one of the most singular of all Spain's rural corners.

**Casares de
las Hurdes**

Natives refer to tiny Casares de las Hurdes as *la capital*. From villages such as this, most of the able-bodied men departed, usually to Switzerland, in the 50s and 60s, leaving behind a population of women, children and old men to tend the fruit trees. The only work now for young people is in the pine forest above or labouring for the local council. You will see such sights as modern tennis courts in some villages, contributions from regional and local government struggling to make good the ravages of age-old poverty. But essentially the system is as it was before – most people have to leave the valley, even if only seasonally, for work.

Huetre
(detour)

Three km on from Casares a 4-km diversion ② to the village of Huetre will give you a feel for Las Hurdes. Leave your car on entering among the few new buildings (erected by returning exiles) and walk on into the medieval muddle of higgledy-piggledy lanes. The houses are made of rough slate slabs laid sideways and casually roofed in immense flat slates as if great shoals of them had swum up to roof level and expired there.

El Gasco
(detour)

Returning to the original road, drop down to Nuñomoral and ③ turn right at the bottom of a steepish slope, by the pension/restaurante El Hurdano. The road, at first unsignposted, soon confirms that it is leading to El Gasco, 9.2 km.

For those in search of deep Las Hurdes, this detour is one of the most promising in the area, up along a narrowing valley, river below, neatly-kept gardens in the small space along its banks. El Gasco, like Huetre, has a few modern houses on entry, but the medievalism is even more striking. The higher part of the old village is composed of slate-built houses, sometimes rounded, with tiny windows and tiny, sunken doors. Most of the houses are now used for animals and you will be pursued by donkey brays and crowing cocks on the far side of closed doors. The best views are from the far end of the village: cross the bridge and climb 100 m or so up the stone path opposite.

Taking photographs of the buildings is no problem, but the villagers themselves are extremely reluctant to be peered at or photographed, wishing to forget the experience of Luis Buñuel coming here to make his famous film, *Tierra sin Pan* (Land Without Bread). King Alfonso XIII also paid a visit to the area. But some people are willing to talk about their lives. "*Mucha montaña y poca tierra*", an old lady said to me, "*sembramos per no recogemos*" – "much mountain, little land; we sow but we cannot harvest."

Returning to Nuñomoral, follow the 'main' road through the rose-grown village of Rubiasco to the junction with the C512, then ④ left to cross the river at Vegas de Coria, a spot where visitors and locals swim in summer. There are pleasant little roadside bars and restaurants for a casual lunch or snack.

Ahead of you now begins to loom an almost perpendicular limestone mountain. *After five miles, turn left ⑤ as signposted for Las Mestas (3 km) and La Alberca (20 km).* Now the road, which has been resurfaced for the last few kilometres, turns old and narrow, running along a valley of great beauty at the foot of the mountain.

Sierra de Francia

At Las Mestas hold right, signposted Las Batuecas, and soon begin the hairpin ascent to La Alberca. Up and up goes the road, twisting through vistas of valley and crag, until finally, 11 km from Las Mestas, most

• *Río Hurdano, El Gasco.*

probably in proximity to wheeling griffon vultures and ravens flying as clumsily as airborne beer bottles, you reach the pass of El Portillo at 1,240 m. On the far side of it, a totally different landscape spreads out, in appearance a wide and undulating plain, though when you are down in it, one that proves extremely hilly, full of secret woods and valleys strewn with granite boulders. To the left rears the peak of La Peña de Francia, ultimate goal of this route. It belongs to the Sierra de Francia, the general name of the district. Away to your right, often snow-covered, is the grander and more austere Sierra de Béjar.

Here, in the more open and friendly land of the Sierra de Francia, the principal glory is the villages which lurk among woods, lie along ridges or crown the tops of hills. Given the change of landscape and building materials, the vernacular architecture is naturally different. Lower storeys are generally composed of substantial chunks of granite, turning to a half-timbered construction above, with small granite stones thrust tightly in between the beams like marbles in a jar. The first floor often reaches out on wooden beams and there will probably be a

• *Arcaded houses, La Alberca.*

wooden balcony, the mauve and red of its geraniums jangling against the lichen-speckled pink of the Roman tiles above.

La Alberca

La Alberca is the first such village (see above) which the road reaches. Being a famous beauty spot it is often full of tourists, with shops and stalls on entry selling honey, locally made wafers or *obleas* the size of dinner plates, pottery and hams. Don't be put off, but walk on up the few metres to the square, with wiggly houses rising above granite arcades and a tall and sombre crucifix in the centre. Here you could try the Bar Moderno for a glimpse of an older, more threadbare Spain with old men playing cards in the dim light. Do wander the side lanes as well, finding alleyways where cobbles turn to living rock and water plashes out of pipes into granite water troughs.

Paris
(hotel/ restaurant, La Alberca)

Of Alberca's three hotels, the friendly Paris is especially recommendable, with comfortable, suprisingly large beds and a restaurant serving such local specialities as *alubias de la Alberca*, which are the much-appreciated white beans grown around the village, with chorizo and pig's ear. *C/ San Antonio, s/n; tel 41 51 31; restaurant price band A/B.*

In La Alberca ⑥ pick up signs for Mogarraz, just in front of the Hotel Paris.

Mogarraz

A linear village, in Alberca style, hung along the hillside underneath the through-road. "People are waking up again, making the corners beautiful", says a man in his 40s in blue overalls, gesturing towards

•*Mogarraz.*

flowers and ancient stone-work. "But there are only four men here who are younger than me".

Mirasierra
(restaurant, Mogarraz)

This popular restaurant – book at weekends – specializes in local dishes such as *patatas meneadas*, literally meaning shaken potatoes, also roasted lamb and kid. Fine sierra views, as you would expect. *On main road; tel 418 144; closed Mon; price band A/B.*

Two to three km further down, keep right for ⑦ Miranda del Castañar if you want to make the detour described below – about 18 km return.

Miranda del Castañar
(detour)

Miranda may well be the loveliest village of the whole route. Largely by-passed by tourists in favour of La Alberca, the modern 'capital', it was Miranda del Castañar which was originally chief settlement after this land was recovered from the Moors in the 13thC. It became a frontier fortress, explaining the four-square castle and handful of seigniorial houses.

Las Petronilas
(bar/fonda, Miranda del Castañar)

There is a fairly routine *hostal* on the slope leading up to the village, with en suite bathrooms, but to my mind this place, on the approach to the castle, better suits Miranda. Old-fashioned, spotlessly clean, though with shared bathrooms, the fonda is friendly and decidedly economical. Good, simple meals are served in the adjoining bar/dining room. *Price band A.*

Retrace (9 km of uphill driving) and ⑧ take the right hand fork for San Martín del Castañar and Las Casas del Conde.

• *The sanctuary church of La Peña de Francia.*

The road winds down and up through woods and vines to Casas del Conde. Turn left and in 2 km arrive at San Martín, lying along a ridge with another castle at the far end. This village, too, is in La Alberca/Miranda del Castañar style.

La Peña de Francia

Carry on about 6 km to El Casarito, a T-junction with the main road into La Alberca. Turn right and immediately left, and left again after 1 km for La Peña de Francia. You have a marvellous climb of 11 km up the side of this famous sanctuary-peak. The final stages begin with a kind of pass — by the name Los Lobos, or the Wolves — at 1,499 m. Then the road winds right round the Peña, offering a tremendous panorama of the scree-clad valley leading down to Ciudad Rodrigo, of a great expanse of Salamanca cattle country and, next, over the very countryside you have just travelled through. The last view of all, when you have safely parked, includes El Portillo, the mountain lip over which you passed to enter this magical country.

Up here you feel as lofty as an angel, and it's no surprise, despite a rocket-shaped communications mast, that this remains a major place of pilgrimage. There's a stern old monastery building, a fairly stern hostel for pilgrims (meals are also served here) and best of all, inside the church, the image of the Virgin of La Peña and her Holy Child, both vivid figures with faces of gleaming, ebony black.

Descending ⑨ around the peak, turn right at the Los Lobos gap. Drop down through the screes on a very narrow, generally unprotected road for Ciudad Rodrigo. After 16 km, the road bumps through the village of Monsagro, then wanders on to Serradilla del Arroyo. Here you will see at once that building styles have returned to Spanish everyday. A final descent leads through the *pata negra* territory back to Ciudad Rodrigo.

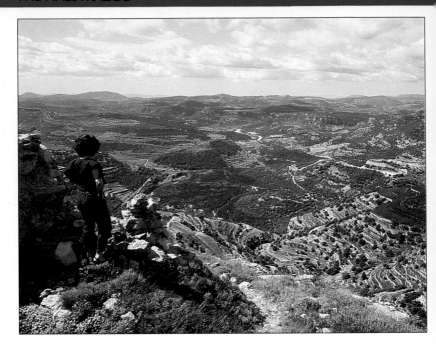

• *View of the Maestrazgo from Ares del Maestre*

For an area so wild, remote and sparsely populated, the Maestrazgo has seen more than its share of battles. Many of El Cid's exploits, fighting for Christians or Moors, depending on where his allegiance lay, took place in these parts. One of his great successes was the storming of Morella in 1084 (when siding with the Christians). One hundred and fifty years later James I, 'the Conqueror', had the first of his victories here during the re-Conquest and many of the villages hereabouts were fortified.

The landscape is fascinating, a plateau cut deep with gorges, and hillsides with extensive terraced fields giving a strange rippled effect. Evening light makes it especially beautiful. Everything about the area is medieval: the landscape, the villages, even some of the farming techniques, and to some extent the roads too.

So far, tourism has had little impact, which is fine if you like to be away from people, and don't mind a scarcity of restaurants.

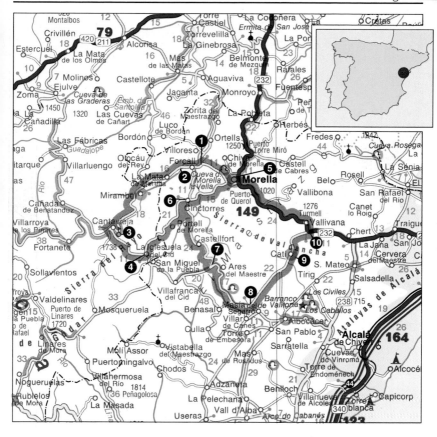

One or two are recommended here, but you may prefer to pack a picnic.

Don't be alarmed by frequently seeing snakes on the road. The long green ones are harmless; the shorter grey ones, much rarer, should be avoided.

ROUTE ONE: 94 KM

Morella

In every sense, Morella's position at the heart of the Maestrazgo is outstanding. Wrapped around a cone-shaped rocky hill like a pink bib, with the castle ruins its crowning glory, it lies within walls, still in excellent condition and complete with 14 towers and four gateways, built in the 14thC by the Knights of Montesa to protect the citizens

• *Plaza Mayor, Forcall.*

from the Moors. The views from the castle are superb and show clearly how the village is surrounded by a ring of hills. Look, too, for the Gothic aqueduct, built in the 14thC.

At the foot of the castle, the ruined San Francisco monastery with its elegant cloisters is undergoing restoration, while a little lower on the hill the Basilica of Santa Maria la Mayor has two fine portals and an unusual raised chancel reached by a carved Renaissance spiral staircase. The Calle Mayor is the best of the medieval streets, especially at the upper end where arcades lead to the old cardinal's palace, which until it closed recently was the best of several hotels in the village. It is hoped eventually to restore the building and re-open it as an hotel. An avenue skirting the northern part of the hill is popular with locals for the evening *paseo*. Of the town's festivals, the most famous is Sexeni, which is celebrated in August every six years (1994, 2000 and so on) in honour of the Virgen de Vallivana which was brought to Morella in the 17thC and is said to have saved the village from the plague. A smaller version of the festival is held at the same time in the preceding year as a kind of dress rehearsal.

• The medieval fortified town, Morella.

Rey Don Jaime *(hotel, Morella)*

Since the closure of the Cardinal Ram, this is the best hotel in town, a modern three-star establishment in the Calle Mayor which blends reasonably well with its much older surroundings. Some of the rooms have fine views of the Maestrazgo. Soft furnishings are in traditional fabrics that have been produced by hand in Morella since the Middle Ages. *Tel 964 16 09 11; price band B/C.*

The Elias, within the walls near the church, though marginally cheaper, doesn't seem to offer the same value; *tel 964 16 00 92.* The Muralla, by the town walls, has basic accommodation at an economical price; *tel 964 16 02 43.*

La Roque *(restaurant, Morella)*

This friendly restaurant, just along the road from the Rey Don Jaime in Segura Barreda and likewise decorated in traditional Morella style, offers local cuisine alongside regular fare. *Tel 964 16 03 36; closed Nov; price band A.*

Leave Morella in the direction of Forcall by a road winding along the foot of some stunning cliff scenery. It was here that the first inhabitants of the region are said to have lived, as evidenced by prehistoric cave paintings nearby. ① Beyond the cliffs, turn left to Forcall, which lies in the valley before you. Just before the village, notice the Ermita Nuestra Senora de la Consolacion standing on a spur above the road.

Forcall

The church is a mixture of Romanesque and 13thC Gothic and as you walk into the interior darkness, your eyes are immediately drawn to two stained glass windows depicting the Virgin, high over the altar. As you grow more accustomed to the dark, you'll become aware of some

• *Todolella castle.*

fine frescos on the ceiling above the altar. Nearby, a splendid medieval mansion, the Palacio de los Osset, in the rectangular and porticoed Plaza Mayor, has recently undergone major restoration.

Meson de la Vila
(*restaurant, Forcall*)

Housed in an unusual building in some ways recalling the Alamo, this restaurant, open all day, is a popular haunt of locals, not surprisingly when you see the extent of the menu and the economical prices. Some of the local specialities worth trying are *pichon, perdiz* or *salmonetes* (pigeon, partridge or mullet). *Tel 964 17 11 25; price band A.*

From Forcall, head along a poppy-filled, rocky valley for Todolella and La Mata. ② *Cross the Rio Cantavieja and immediately turn right at the T-junction for Todolella.*

Todolella
(*detour*)

Just a couple of kilometres off the main route, Todolella is an attractive medieval village best known for its castle, which has been handsomely restored and is now a private residence.

Return to the T-junction at the Rio Cantavieja, then carry straight on to La Mata, which lies just off the road and has little of interest to detain you. Continue along the narrow but fertile valley of the Cantavieja to a bridge at the border between the provinces of Castellon and Teruel, where turn left towards Mirambel.

Mirambel
A medieval walled village lying just off the road, Mirambel has won awards for the quality of its restoration. You enter through the Europa-Nostra gateway which leads past a tower to the cobbled streets where grand mansions of the 15th, 16th and 17thC stand beside balconied and galleried houses. A place like this, practically anywhere else in Europe, would be over-run with tourists. Here in hidden Spain you'll have it almost entirely to yourself apart from the few inhabitants. If you would like to stay overnight there is a *fonda* – from outside it looks no more than a low-key bar – in the main street. All the rooms at the Guimera have recently been modernised and improved to a higher-than-average level of comfort; yet prices are modest. *Tel 964 17 82 69.*

Beyond Mirambel, the road winds through beautiful scenery. In about 12 km the village of Cantavieja suddenly looms ahead in its dramatic cliff-top location. As the road winds uphill, fabulous views stretch back down the valley you've just driven along, then as you round the bluff on which the village stands, a much wilder mountain panorama opens up.

Cantavieja
The best part of this village is the porticoed Plaza de Cristo Rey with its escutcheoned buildings, among which is the *ayuntamiento*. Through an arch at the back of the square, there is another fine view down the valley, which you can now enjoy at your leisure if you weren't able to appreciate it on the drive up. The church at one side of the square has an octagonal clock tower that is slightly separate and which forms a gateway across the road.

③ *From Cantavieja take the road signposted La Iglesuela del Cid, which winds along the edge of a limestone gorge with glorious views. As you approach La Iglesuela, the scenery takes on a deep golden hue from the stones used in the network of drystone walls. Just before arriving in the village note the turning to the left for Cinctorres and Morella which you'll need when leaving.*

La Iglesuela del Cid
The name recalls the exploits of the legendary El Cid in this area during the 11thC, which led ultimately to his capture of Valencia in 1094. There are several large 15thC and 16thC mansions, a 13thC town hall in the porticoed Plaza de la Iglesia, a church with an attractively decorated dome and a richly ornate chapel in Baroque style.

④ *Take the road to Cinctorres and Morella, driving out past terraced* fields and ochre drystone walls, gently climbing to the Puerto de las Cabrillas, 1,320 metres. It is a bleak landscape up here, where farmers still use horse-drawn ploughs, and the wind creates weird wave formations through the grassy fields. In winter it is horribly inhospitable, but in summer it has a rugged beauty. Beyond the pass, you drop down past limestone cliffs and the terraced hillsides that are so typical of the Maestrazgo, while far away in the distance you can see Morella standing proud, some 30 km as the crow flies.

Beyond Puerto la Morella, the road follows a winding route down through limestone ravines with more stupendous views. In a few more kilometres, Cinctorres suddenly appears ahead.

Cinctorres
Dominated by the huge twin octagonal belfries of the 17thC church of Sant Pere, Cinctorres is a tranquil village on the verge of breaking into tourism, with the 15thC Palace of Sant Joans being converted into a hotel. The little Ermita de Sant Lluis has a delightful painted ceiling, though your best view may only be through the small window in the door.

Depart from Cinctorres in the direction of Morella which appears and disappears frequently as the road twists and undulates through the hills. Finally you crest the rim of hills surrounding Morella and make your way back up to the ancient walls.

ROUTE TWO: III KM

Set out from Morella on the Forcall road again, but in little more than a kilometre fork left for Cinctorres ⑤. *There, follow the signs initially for La Iglesuela del Cid but at the edge of the village fork left for Castellfort* ⑥. The road is narrow and winding but passes through some outstanding wild scenery, and though the going is slow, it's all the better for appreciating the landscape.

Castellfort
Understandably for a remote mountain village such as this, the locals tend to eye strangers with suspicion. There is little to encourage people to stop, but some of the houses have appealing tiled picture panels on the walls. There are also magnificent panoramas of the surrounding terraced hills.

Drystone walls are a feature of the landscape after Castellfort, while the road climbs to a high point of 1,275m at the Port de Sant Pere. *From here follow the road signposted Castellon, winding downhill past the 16thC Hospideria y Ermita Mare de Deu de la Font. The road levels and straightens out and shortly reaches an unsignposted T-junction, where* ⑦ *turn left.* If you have been planning to picnic, the stretch of road from Castellfort to this junction has plenty of opportunities. Soon turn left again to drive up to Ares del Maestre.

• *Santurio Nuestra Señora, La Avellá.*

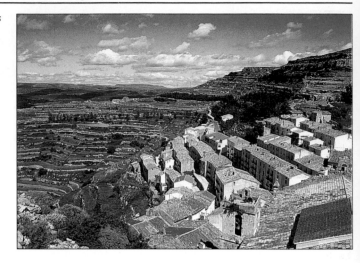

Ares del Maestre

A one-time bastion of the Muslim kingdom of Valencia, this is Morella in miniature, its houses huddled round a rocky summit in much the same way as its neighbour. Sadly, only a few stones remain of the castle that stood at the top of the hill from the 8thC. Take the footpath up to get the commanding views of the Maestrazgo which the defenders of old must have appreciated. It was here that James I achieved an unexpectedly quick victory when he captured the stronghold from the Moors in January 1232 during the re-conquest of Valencia. In the village itself, attractive Gothic-Mudéjar arches stand beside the small *ayuntamiento*, while in the Plaza Mayor one of the old balconied buildings is undergoing conversion into an hotel.

Return to the main road at the foot of the hill.

Meson el Coll

(*restaurant, Ares del Maestre*)

A simple restaurant at the junction of the main road and the village turn-off, and one of very few in this area, a rare opportunity in these parts to sit down and eat in cool comfort. The menu changes daily but there is also a choice of light dishes from the tapas bar. *Tel 964 44 16 85; price band A.*

Continue in the direction of La Pobla Torresa and in about 7 km arrive at Montalbana.

Montalbana

This tiny hamlet consists of little more than a bar, but the bar provides access to a vast gallery of wall paintings dating back to 5000 BC hidden away in the caves of Barranco de Gasulla, about 3 km away. The bar owner is not only the key-holder but the guide to the cave paintings: there are around 300 of them depicting hunters with bows and arrows and their quarry. The tour takes about two hours. Unfortunately, the guide speaks only Spanish, but he doesn't charge a fee — you just tip him whatever seems appropriate. There are a few prehistoric artifacts in showcases in the bar.

Take the road through Montalbana, driving through a wide, flat-bottomed gorge full of olive groves for about 8 km until you see a bridge crossing the river to your right. (8) Just past the bridge (don't cross it) turn left towards Cati, which you reach after about 11 km along a broad valley.

Cati

This village, the liveliest on the route apart from Morella, may surprise you with its 15thC buildings and monuments — chapels, shrines and fountains. The Fuente San Vicente, with a shrine above a spring, is one of the prettiest, while the public washroom opposite is a popular meeting place of the old women, often dressed in their widows' weeds. The village is also known for an excellent cheese.

(9) Just as you leave Cati, turn left on a road signposted La Avellá and wind uphill 3 km or so, as far as the road goes.

La Avellá
(*detour*)

A tiny village overlooking a natural bowl in the hills, La Avellá is worth the excursion just to see its 16thC Sancturio Nuestra Señora de la Avellá. Walk up between two *fondas* to the entrance and inside you'll find the walls and ceilings covered with the most amazing frescos, showing Christ in Majesty and various biblical scenes. The water from a small spring opposite the chapel is said to be a cure for skin diseases. *Drive back down to the main road at Cati and turn left, continuing about another 8 km to the T-junction with the Vinaros-Zaragoza road, where (10) turn left for Morella.*

Vallivana

The Virgen de Vallivana, said to have saved Morella from the plague, came from here. The village lies just to the left of the main road in what almost amounts to a lay-by. Next to the church is an interesting inn, the Parador Vallivana, not in fact part of the state-owned hotel chain, but an independent and popular stop for travellers in the know. It has a huge dining room where people sit down to meals at massive stone tables.

Return to the main road, heading for Morella. On this approach you get the best view of the town, just beyond what looks like a monument standing on the hillside to the right. In fact it is only a pedestal, all that remains of a large statue of Christ which was destroyed when the farmer on whose land it stood was killed by communists during the Civil War.

Drive on until you eventually reach Morella.

• Above, the eerie limestone sculptures of the Ciudad Encantada.

• Inset right, Mural, Huélamo.

'City of surprises' is a fair enough tag for Cuenca: it is certainly a place to spend many an hour, walking back into history, happening upon interesting corners and amazing views. But the Serrania de Cuenca, to the north of the city, is even more of a surprise: a total contrast to the parched plains to the south.

This is green Spain, with a capital G. Mountains and forests predominate and human habitation is scarce. Instead of watching village life go by, you will be treading softly, watching for the wildlife: deer, wild boar, red squirrels, butterflies, eagles and vultures, wild flowers. Some of the scenery is extraordinary – for example the Júcar Gorge above Salto de Villalba; the source of the Rio Cuervo; or the Ciudad Encantada. You will want to get out of the car and walk in order to appreciate these.

The Serrania de Cuenca is a large area which deserves several days to explore; the route shown here is just right for two days.

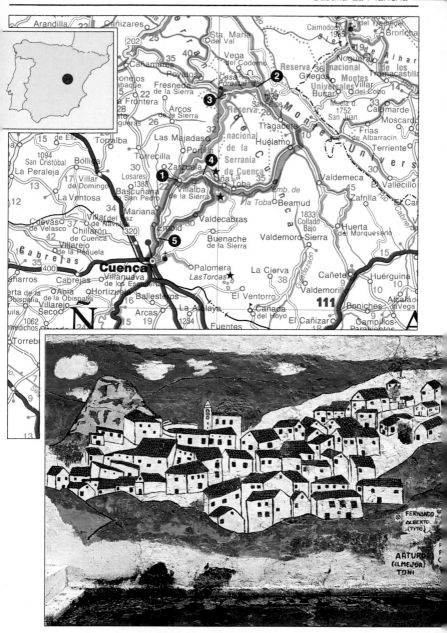

ROUTE: 166 KM

Cuenca

This settlement of 40,000 people is essentially two towns in one. Down at the edge of the plain is the bustling modern town, while high on the plateau is the medieval quarter, by far the most interesting part. It's easy to understand why Cuenca's founders chose this spot, a superb defensive position, almost surrounded by the deep gorges of the Huécar and Júcar rivers. Ground space was limited and as the population grew they had to build upwards, creating medieval skyscrapers up to 12 storeys high. These houses, many of them colour washed, are perched right at the edge of the cliff creating a spectacular skyline. A small group of them with wooden balconies, suspended perilously hundreds of feet above the Huécar, are known as the Casas Colgadas, the hanging houses. One has become a popular restaurant, while its neighbour is home to a museum of abstract art.

Just behind these stands the cathedral, a strange mixture of Gothic, Renaissance, French and Norman architecture made even more complicated by a partial collapse of the west front early this century. You can drive along cobbled streets up to the old town, entering the cathedral square through an arch beneath the 18thC *ayuntamiento*. There is meter parking in the square, also a number of restaurants and bars to suit all tastes and pockets, and shops selling ceramics catering largely for less discriminating tastes.

Parador de Cuenca
(hotel/ restaurant, Cuenca)

Opened in April 1993, this parador is located in the 16thC San Pablo convent facing Cuenca from its lofty perch on the edge of the Huécar Gorge. It's expensive, but with highly comfortable rooms and exceptional views of Cuenca, you may well think it worthwhile. There is also handy access to the old town by way of a footbridge over the gorge.

The restaurant, which has a beautifully carved ceiling, offers typical Cuencan cuisine such as *ajo arriero* (fish in a garlic sauce of tomatoes and hot peppers) and *morteruelo* (pork liver cooked with giblets and game in a variety of spices). *Tel 966 23 23 20; price band B.*

A useful alternative to the parador in the old town is the three-star Leonor de Aquitania, which also has fine views over the gorge. Only marginally cheaper, it has some lovely beamed rooms and a vaulted restaurant in the basement. *Tel 966 23 10 00; price band B.* For cheaper places, best look in the lower town where there is a wide choice.

Meson Casas Colgadas
(restaurant, Cuenca)

To go to Cuenca and not at least enter this 15thC building is to miss one of the town's best experiences. The beautifully timbered interior and striking views can make it difficult to concentrate on the food. Try the *caldereta de cordero* (lamb stew) and the *queso Manchego con miel* (ewe's cheese with honey).

• *Cuenca.*

The only minus point is the piped muzack. If you want to take a look inside and enjoy the dizzy views without eating, there is a downstairs bar which is just as atmospheric. *Tel 966 22 35 09; closed Tues eve; price band B.*

Take the road out of Cuenca following the signs for Ciudad Encantada, driving initially through the Júcar Gorge beneath red and black streaked limestone cliffs. About 4 km from Cuenca you'll pass a ceramics workshop called Alfar Iberico whose pottery is far more attractive, and typical of the region, than that found in many of the shops in Cuenca. Shortly after, your road passes under a bridge carrying the road to Valdecabras. *Just before Villalba de la Sierra ① the road divides: bear right towards Tragacete.* Immediately the scene changes as the road winds up into the hills, passing the small, modern village of Salto de Villalba which comprises a church, several houses and a hydro-electric station, all built in the same strangely attractive style. A few bends farther on, you reach the Ventano del Diablo.

Ventano del Diablo   The Devil's Window is a natural arch in the limestone cliffs which tower above the Rio Júcar. There are views down on to the green, limpid water of the river as it gushes through the gorge hundreds of feet below.

• *Embalse de la Toba.*

• *The sleepy village of Huélamo.*

The road continues to climb, giving views of the plain and the Júcar Gorge. *At the T-junction where the Ciudad Encantada is signposted to the right, carry on towards Tragacete.* A little farther on a section of old road to the left forms a lay-by where you can stop to admire the spectacular rock formations of the gorge.

Uña

This small, peaceful village beside a lake is a useful place to stop at if you're looking for lunch – there is a choice of three restaurants. The Zaballos is the first you'll notice as you enter the village, a cool place with a rustic feel and good home-style cooking. *Tel 966 28 13 02; price band A.* Next door, La Laguna is much the same, but serves lunch only, and in slightly less rustic atmosphere. *Tel 966 28 14 96; price band A.* The third option is found across the road in the village itself, at the Hotel Agua Riscos, a charming and modestly priced little place with a shady walled and terraced courtyard. *Tel 966 28 13 32; price band A. Drive on, arriving in about 5 km at the Embalse de la Toba.*

Embalse de la Toba

Part of the hydro-electric scheme operating on the Júcar, this artificial lake, its waters a deep turquoise colour, blends in well with the rocky outcrops and pine-covered hills surrounding it. La Toba, a small holiday village standing at the head of the lake, is for the exclusive use of people working for the electricity company, but there are plenty of opportunities to stop elsewhere by the lake to picnic or fish.

From La Toba, the road hugs first the lake shore and then the river, narrower now, though the valley is wider. After 15 km or so, Huélamo, off to the right, can be seen strung round the slope high on the hillside.

Huélamo

Stillness pervades. Sheep wander the fields, while at a little mirador an

artist has painted a fetching view of the village on a wall beside a spring. The church stands at one end beside a curious rocky outcrop from where there is another view over the village. You'll also find two bars.
Return to the main road and turn right for Tragacete, about 10 km.

Tragacete

A strange place: a series of small squares are linked by little streets. It is described as a holiday resort, though the major part of its income is from forestry. Holiday makers come here for peaceful breaks and to get close to nature – there is plenty of walking and fishing.

One worthwhile walk is to the top of Cerro de San Felipe (1,839 metres) and back, about four hours. Don't attempt it without a suitable map of the area, showing the footpaths; and don't rely on finding a map in Tragacete – buy in Cuenca. Some of the hotels can loan guide books, but these of course are in Spanish. The path to San Felipe starts from the San Blas youth hostel, signposted from the road skirting the village. A small supermarket in the village is useful for picnic supplies.

Serrania
(hotel,
Tragacete)

Though quite small, Tragacete is the largest place on this part of the route, with several hotels and pensions. It is situated about half way round the circuit, ideal for an overnight stop. The Serrania is modern, with carved timber balconies giving it the look of a mountain hotel. It is pretty inside, and moderately priced; it also has a delightful little restaurant. *Tel 966 28 90 19.*

Other hotels worth considering and similarly priced are the neighbouring Júcar *tel 966 28 90 16,* and the El Gamo *tel 966 28 90 08.* The latter is in the main square. Both have their own restaurants. All three restaurants are in *price band A.*

Leaving Tragacete, continue along the valley 12 km through fine mountain scenery, along pine-clad valleys and past limestone cliffs that thrust spectacularly above the greenery, until you reach the car park for the Nacimiento del Cuervo, to the right of the road opposite a roadside café and bar.

Nacimiento del Cuervo

The Rio Cuervo is an insignificant river compared to its neighbour the Tajo, better known as the Tagus when it reaches the Atlantic near Lisbon, but its source is much more appealing. A track leads from the car park about 300 metres through woods and alongside the gurgling infant river to a clearing with a crystal pool filled by sparkling threads of water spilling over mossy rocks. It's a delightful spot, with dappled sunlight beneath the pines, red squirrels scurrying among the trees and butterflies of every hue. Chances are you could have it all to yourself, too. It is a superb picnic place. This pool is not actually the source – that is a few hundred metres farther on, and, though not quite so pretty, is worth the effort. To see them at their best, go mid to late afternoon. Some of the water, refreshingly cool, is piped to taps in the car park.

• *Forest road,*
Serrania de
Cuenca.

Leaving the car park, head back towards Tragacete and after about 2 km turn right on to a camino forestal (forest road) beside ② the log cabins of an area recreativa. There are no direction signs. This is a charming road to drive: though narrow, the chance of meeting other traffic is slight. Here is wild Spain at its very best, practically untouched by tourism. The speed limit is 40 kph, but you are unlikely to want to go any faster. The scenery ranges from gentle valleys to wild ravines and there are numerous places where you can pull off the road and wander on foot. From one small mirador on the left, you can descend by steps into a ravine. The area is rich in wild flowers, birds and butterflies: you will wish you had bought fieldguides.

Continue to the Casa Forestal de Tejadillos (the first building you come across since joining the forest road) and ③ turn left towards Las Majadas, Villalba de la Sierra and Cuenca – note the rustic road sign. A series of junctions follows: keep heading in the direction indicated for any of the names that appeared on the earlier sign.

Las Majadas This village, the first you've seen since Tragacete nearly 40 km back, comes as a surprise after the beauty of the last few kilometres. A sleepy place where voices echo off surrounding buildings and dogs lie snoozing in the middle of the square, oblivious of the few passing cars, it is an even more peaceful place in which to stay than Tragacete. There is a *hostal* and a pension from which to choose.

On the outskirts of Las Majadas, follow the signs initially for Los Callejones and almost immediately fork right for Cuenca. As this guide went to press, the road from here on was somewhat pitted, but there are plenty of fine views to compensate, especially to the right towards the Sierra de

• *Ciudad Encantada.*

Bascuñana. Continue on the road's sinuous descent to Villalba de la Sierra.

Villalba de la Sierra

A fairly large village, Villalba has a number of shops for picnic supplies. Note the funny little church with its stunted tower.

Take the road towards Cuenca, then at the T-junction just outside the village turn left for Tragacete and the Ciudad Encantada. You now repeat an 8-km stretch covered on Route One, going past the Ventano del Diablo until the right turn ④ to Ciudad Encantada; take it.

Ciudad Encantada

An extensive area of fantastic limestone shapes sculpted by water and weather, the Enchanted City is an eerie place to wander in alone, especially when the wind is blowing through the pines. There is a modest entry charge and a guide book is recommended since it points out many of the most important formations on a 3-km circuit. The gigantic shapes are given names such as Los Barcos, which look like ships lying alongside each other; El Crocodilo y el Elefante (a crocodile and elephant facing up to each other) or Cara del Hombre (a man's face); but there is also plenty of scope for using your imagination.

Elsewhere a 200-metre narrow passageway called El Tobogan looks like a toboggan run, which emerges at the Mar de Piedra (sea of stone), a limestone pavement that in places looks like the surface of the moon. Though the area is popular at times with school groups and other tourists, it is usually easy enough to escape them and you could just as likely be sharing your visit with squirrels, lizards and bell-clanking ponies. A rustic bar at the entrance serves a variety of *bocadillos* and cheap meals, and if you feel so inclined you could buy a whole Manchego cheese.

Across the road, the modern Hostal Ciudad Encantada has rooms – quite reasonably priced most of the year, though with a premium in July and August – plus a restaurant that offers a menu featuring local specialities and wine. *Tel 966 28 81 94; price band A.* If walking around the Enchanted City hasn't been enough for you, a path behind the hotel will take you 1.8 km to the Mirador de Uña where you can look down on the Júcar Valley.

The road continues through pine forest and then descends through more rugged country into the valley. Down below you can see Valdecabras gathered round its large square church and though you could pull in there to experience more village life, there is nothing special to delay you.

Farther on, the road descends through a gorge and then crosses the Rio Júcar before ⑤ *rejoining the road through the Hoz de Júcar back to Cuenca.*

Just after Cuenca comes into view, take a left turn signposted Sancturio de las Angustias, driving uphill as far as you can go, then walking up steps to the pretty little chapel. Strangely, the normal silence of a chapel is broken here by the ticking of a loud clock. There is a fine statue of Christ and the Virgin and from the terrace there are views of the gorge. It can also be reached on foot from old Cuenca. Back down the hill and just before re-crossing the Júcar and taking the road back to Cuenca, there's a pleasant little terraced bar by the shady riverside.

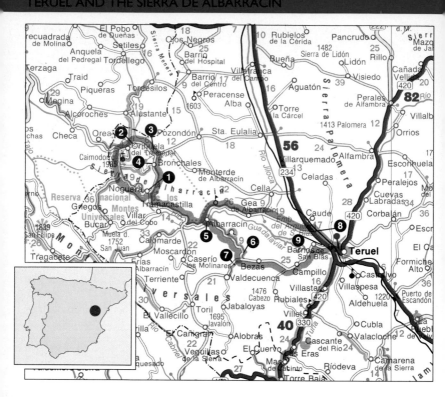

The landscape around Teruel takes on a wonderful variety of shapes and colours, ranging from the impressive grandeur of the Albarracin mountain country to the arid plains and reddish desert near Teruel. The Moorish influence was very strong here, especially in the buildings, and even after the Christians under Alfonso II of Aragon re-conquered the region in 1171, the Moors were permitted to live alongside in peace. One result of this co-habitation was Mudéjar architecture of which Teruel has some of the finest examples in all Spain.

Albarracin, another former stronghold of the Moors and one of the prettiest places in the whole of Aragon, lies between the desert and the mountains and is a useful springboard for both. The greenery of the *sierra* to the west makes a welcome contrast to the shimmering plain on the way to Teruel. Like much of mountainous Spain it is remote, and many villagers, even in the small summer resorts of Bronchales and Orihuela

• *Part of the defensive wall around Albarracin.*

del Tremedal, seem to view strangers with some suspicion and curiosity.

This is an area that must be enjoyed at a slow pace: the narrow, snaking roads will slow you right down. When you get to Teruel and Albarracin, wander at leisure. There is much to absorb, and in any case, the way of life here is rather less than hurried.

ROUTE ONE: 86 KM

Albarracin   One-time capital of a Moorish state called Azagras, Albarracin occupies a wonderful position tucked into the hillside above the Río Guadalaviar, and is full of almost perfectly preserved medieval streets of peach-washed timber-framed houses with projecting wooden balconies. You can get a fine view of the town in its setting from the old defensive walls built up the steep hill behind. There is another view from a terrace in front of the cathedral.

The cathedral itself is an attractive building with colourful glazed tiles on the roof of its tower, while its treasury contains six tapestries that were made in Brussels around the same time the cathedral was rebuilt

• *Albarracin, an almost perfectly preserved medieval town.*

in the 16thC. This is one of the most picturesque towns in Aragon, every bend in the narrow streets revealing another gem. There are one or two souvenir shops selling mainly ceramics of reasonable quality produced by local artisans, plus a few bars and restaurants. A couple of bars in the Plaza Mayor are particularly atmospheric, notably the Aben Razin, named after an 11thC dynasty from which the town gets its name. The nearby La Taberna offers interesting snacks.

Albarracin
(*hotel,
Albarracin*)

This is the best and by far the priciest hotel in town, but if you want to take in some of the atmosphere of your surroundings this is the place to stay since it is one of the original old mansions. *Tel 974 71 00 11; price band B.*

If you want something more modest, the family-run Hostal Olimpia stands on the road skirting the old centre. The rooms, though small, are comfortable and there is a restaurant which serves the simple food typical of the region. Although it is on the main road past the village, you're more likely to be disturbed by the clanking bells of sheep being driven past rather than traffic. *Tel 974 71 00 83; price band A.*

Rincon del Chorro
(*restaurant, Albarracin*)

In one of the steep, narrow lanes leading up to the Plaza Mayor, this first-floor restaurant with a balcony overlooking the street is run by a big, friendly giant named Pedro Narro Sáez. He serves up portions in keeping with his size. A delicious and substantial meal on its own is *Entremeses Arogoneses,* a starter with three kinds of sausage and cured ham. A recommendable main course is *Lengha Estofada* (tongue stew). If you would like something less filling, try the tapas bar downstairs. *Tel 974 71 01 12; closed Sun and Mon, also Mon-Thur from Jan to Mar; price band A/B.*

Follow the road around the foot of the town and pass through the tunnel beneath the cathedral, heading for Torres de Albarracin and Orihuela del Tremedal. The road is accompanied by the Guadalaviar through a narrow gorge with overhanging rock faces; there are several places where you can stop and admire the grandeur. Eventually you spill out into a wider valley cutting into the Sierra de Albarracin, here sparsely planted with conifers. *Follow the signs for Orihuela, then Torres de Albarracin,* a small farming community containing a jumble of houses around a ramshackle church of red stone. *In another 4 km you reach Tramacastilla which you enter by turning left by a small roadside chapel.*

Tramacastilla
A mixture of old and new houses, Tramacastilla is much neater than Torres de Albarracin, and feels more friendly. It is not far from its neighbour, but its setting in a narrow part of the valley is much more attractive; and you are on the doorstep of some of the most rugged country in Spain. A pleasant touch is the street names displayed by means of colourful ceramic bowls set into the walls.

As you leave Tramacastilla, the road begins to climb and you have a view that reveals the village's wild location. *Carry on into Noguera ①.*

Noguera
This village stands wedged between two bare hillsides, with a large square church and old stone houses gathered around it. Sounds seem to be magnified here by the hills: the chattering of birds is particularly noticeable until the church bells take over, echoing loudly around the buildings. You'll also notice the aroma of *fabada* wafting from kitchens if you wander about just before lunch.

The road snakes round the edge of Noguera, then narrows as it climbs through pine woods, where you might see red deer. The area is also known for its rare butterflies and wild flowers. At the top of the climb, at the Virgen del Carmen, a small roadside shrine, there are grassy slopes looking out across the mountains: ideal for picnics. From

• *The spa
village
Bronchales.*

here the road widens a little and skirts the mountain providing splendid panoramas of the Montes Universales. Farther on there are even more opportunities to pull off for a picnic in the pine forests. In some places there is spring water, too. *Continue through the forest, ignoring the right turn to Bronchales at the Puerto Orihuela and descend to Orihuela de Tremedal.*

Orihuela de Tremedal

The church of San Millan overlooks tiers of pantiled roofs and charming balconies. It is simple from outside, but there is a magnificent Baroque interior, refreshingly bright, with ornate arches, pillars and capitals.

Los Pinares
(*hotel,
Orihuela de
Tremedal*)

This modern whitewashed hotel is your first sight of the village as the road leaves the forest. The rooms are very comfortable and quite reasonably priced. Restaurant and bar have hunting trophies mounted on the walls. *Tel 974 71 42 98; price band A.*

Cheaper but much less comfortable accommodation is available in the village centre at the Hostal Espinosa and the Bar Oriola.

Before leaving Orihuela turn right off the main road to visit the Ermita Virgen del Tremedal, a little less than 5 km away along a rough forest track. The *ermita* itself is abandoned and locked but it is in a wonderful position with superb views northwards over Orihuela and far beyond. Grassy slopes make it popular with Spanish families for weekend picnics, and if you want to do the same but in isolation you need wander no more than 200 m or so from the car to find a suitable spot, either in the sun or the shade.

Back at the main road, ②, follow the signs for Zaragoza and Teruel, essentially keeping to the road ahead. The scenery is very different from that before Orihuela, the pine forests being replaced by scrubby open countryside while the road now follows a straight course. ③ *After about 6 km turn right for Bronchales.*

Bronchales   A sprawling spa village of whitewashed walls and pink pantiled roofs overlooked by a hill-top chapel. Old men, viewing strangers with an ambiguous mixture of indifference and curiosity, sit in the sun on benches in front of the 16thC church, or under the trees in the main square; the women peer from dark doorways. There are a couple of bars, but be prepared for the stares.

④ *From Bronchales, follow the signs for Albarracin, Las Palomas and then Noguera.* Take this section slowly in order to appreciate fully the mountain panoramas spreading to the east. At ① *On the outskirts of Noguera turn left towards Albarracin and Teruel and repeat the first part of the route,* this time with views in the opposite direction, increasing your appreciation of the Guadalaviar Gorge.

■■■■■■■ # ROUTE TWO: 85 KM

⑤ *Opposite the Hostal Olimpia in Albarracin take the turning signposted Bezas.*

Shortly after Arrabal Santa Barbara, park on the grass to the left for a visit to the Fuente del Cabrerizo. A path leads to the top of a pine-clad gorge of red stone and steps go down to the spring and a lovely woodland walk. In another kilometre along the road you come to a delightful picnic area among the trees (very popular on summer weekends) that was once the home of prehistoric man. More woodland walks lead to caves and rocky corners where works of art depicting men and animals painted around 6000 BC are still visible on the stone walls. Poster panels at the picnic area provide information (in Spanish) about the pictures.

Beyond here the road is narrow and quite pot-holed, but there is some tremendous scenery with frequent jagged rock faces projecting out of the pine forests.

⑥ *At a crossroads in the forest bear right for Bezas via Domaque. (The route ahead, also signposted Bezas, is no more than a rough track and best avoided.) Approaching Bezas, the road winds through forests then, at a T-junction, turn left* ⑦ *for Teruel and Bezas.* Just before Bezas, the conifers and rocky outcrops are left behind and a much gentler landscape takes its place.

Bezas   The village lies just off the road to the left. It has little to attract the passing traveller, but cast a glance at the pretty little church with

• *Los Arcos aqueduct, Teruel. (above)*   • *El Salvador tower, Teruel. (right)*

coloured tiles capping its belfry.

El Campillo   This strange looking place has an economy based on agriculture and cattle rearing. The soil is a deep red. On the outskirts are many farm sheds, some of them in various states of ruin. The church, at the edge of the village, with an attractive octagonal belfry, stands reflected in a small fishing pond.

The road continues across the red plain, with occasional rocky outcrops contributing to the desert-like nature of the scenery. After 6 km or so you reach San Blas, another agricultural village with little to offer other than a bar. ⑧ *About 4 km from San Blas, the road reaches the N234: turn right.* There's a modern parador almost opposite (*tel 974 60 18 00*). *In a couple of hundred metres turn left and follow the signs into Teruel.*

Teruel   Although Teruel suffered badly in the Civil War, it has retained much of its Mudéjar architecture, notably in its cathedral and the four remaining towers of its walls. Mudéjar architecture, characterized by

• *Gea de Albarracin.*

intricate brickwork and ceramic decoration, is basically Moorish in concept but flourished during Christian occupation in the Middle Ages. The 12thC cathedral constructed in beautifully worked golden brick blends Romanesque and Renaissance styles with the Mudéjar. Inside, the ceiling is a masterpiece of Gothic-Mudéjar style. The carved altarpiece is the French sculptor Gabriel Joly's finest work. Of the four towers, the best, said to be among the finest in the country, are the San Martin and El Salvador towers, the latter with a vaulted archway allowing traffic to pass beneath.

The church of San Pedro is another fine piece of Mudéjar art, with a story of tragic love attached. Isabel de Segura and Diego de Marcilla lived in the 13thC and though they were in love, Diego was refused Isabel's hand in marriage by her father until he had proved himself. Out he went into the world, but on his return five years later Diego found Isabel had married someone else. He died in despair, and at his funeral she too died of a broken heart. They were buried together, and now lie in an alabaster tomb in a chapel attached to the church. In recent years it has become the object of pilgrimages by newlyweds.

On the edge of the town, one of the lesser known sights is Los

Arcos, a well-preserved 16thC aqueduct which crosses the road from Alfambra.

Reina Cristina
(hotel/ restaurant, Teruel)

A modern hotel just by the El Salvador tower, the Reina Cristina is a comfortable place, but at a higher than average three-star price. The restaurant is excellent, though also somewhat pricey. *Tel 974 60 68 60; price band B.*

From Teruel follow the signs for Zaragoza along the N234, passing the parador again, and in about 6 km ⑨ branch left for Albarracin . The road runs straight as a die for 10 km or more across the cereal-covered plain, its surface shimmering in the heat and the Sierra de Albarracin slowly looming up in the distance. Just after the Cella turning, the road starts to twist and turn as it reaches the edge of the sierra, until eventually you arrive at Gea de Albarracin.

Gea de Albarracin

This village has a number of attractive old houses as well as a large former Carmelite church. The narrow shaded streets make a welcome break from the fierce sun and the sound of the tinkling fountain in the small central square has a delightfully cooling effect.

Shortly after Gea de Albarracin, the road winds through a leafy gorge where you'll find any number of places to pull off for a picnic beside the sparkling Guadalaviar, either in the open or in the shade. At one point about 10 km from Gea you pass castle ruins perched on a cliff to the right and within another 4 km the old walls of Albarracin come into view.

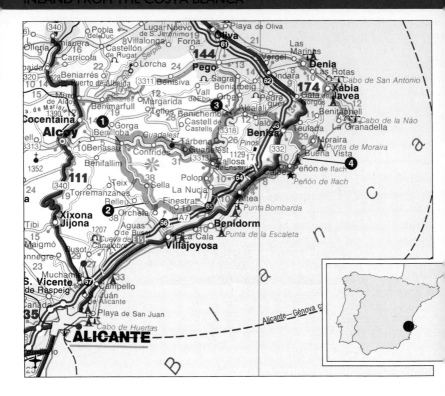

You will probably start this route from Altea, a resort on one of Spain's most popular package holiday destinations; however, the bustle of the beaches is soon behind as you cross spectacular mountain chains behind the coast.

In fact, Altea is more than just another resort. The old town has plenty of atmosphere: a jumble of white houses swarms around a prominent, blue-domed church on the top of a hill, reached only from the seafront far below by steep streets and long flights of steps.

Each of the two loops circles a great mountain range: respectively, the Sierra Aitana (which reaches 1,558 metres) and the Sierra Bernia. The first route also visits Guadalest, one of the most picturesque villages in eastern Spain, and an exquisite but little known garden. The second crosses a rugged pass and returns to the coast via the vineyards of the Jalón valley before passing underneath a rock big enough to rival that of Gibraltar.

• *Man wearing traditional Moorish costume.*

The villages in the mountains are self-contained communities speaking their own language, Valencian – you'll see place names written in both languages. They have plenty of restaurants serving a variety of local dishes to complement the ubiquitous *paella*.

The best month to see this area is February, when the many terraces climbing the mountainsides dance with white and pink almond blossom.

ROUTE ONE: 116 KM

Altea

The lower part of this fishing town is a tourist development, but the attractive old quarter – a labyrinth of alleys, steps and white houses, popular with artists – has not changed at all. The local game *pelota*, in which a ball is struck with the bare hands, is played in the streets on Sundays and fiestas. Cars are not permitted within the old town but there is usually somewhere to park in one of the peripheral streets. Altea's hotels are sandwiched between the main road and the beach. The smartest is Cap Negret (*tel 96 584 12 00*), a large complex with banks of rooms overlooking a seaside swimming pool. If you prefer a smaller, cheaper hotel closer to the town, try Altaya (*tel 96 584 08 00*).

Bodegón de Pepe (*bar-restaurant, Altea*)

There are only three items on the menu in this old-fashioned bar – broad beans, fried fish and mussels – but they are enough for a memorable meal. You are unceremoniously provided with a bucket into which to toss the left-overs. *On the main road, Conde de Altea, close to the traffic lights; no telephone; price band A.*

Leave Altea on the main road, the N332 in the direction of Valencia. After about 3 km take the right turn signposted for the A7 motorway and, in smaller letters, Callosa. Cross the main road and after less than 0.5 km turn right for Callosa. After passing through the village of Altea la Vieja the road runs along the foot of the Sierra Bernia, crossing the River Algar and climbing to reach Callosa.

Callosa de Ensarriá

From a distance, the town, important for the export of medlars, looks uninvitingly modern, but it hides a heart of houses painted in a traditional bright blue colour, one of which has been converted into an art gallery.

Turn left at the roundabout in the town centre for Guadalest. The road follows the valley giving attractive views of the crag-topped Sierra Aitana at every turn. Shortly after leaving Callosa, look out for road-side stalls selling honey. You will be invited to compare different flavours before buying. The road dips down to a bridge to cross the Guadalest river again and then rises through the trees. Ahead appears the castle and belfry of Castell de Guadalest, perched precariously on a rock outcrop.

Castell de Guadalest

Despite the coachloads, Guadalest remains relatively unspoilt because it can only be visited on foot. Leave your car in the car park to the left of the road and take the narrow street opposite which leads to a short sloping tunnel giving access to the single street and square of the old village.

There are fine views over a vivid turquoise-coloured reservoir from the parapet flanking the square.

• *Castell de Guadalest.*

A variety of souvenir/craft shops sell leather, pottery, textiles and green recycled glass. The summit of the rock is occupied by the town cemetery – the highest in Spain – and the castle from which there are all-round views. Guadalest also has a bizarre claim to fame: two museums of microscopic art displaying (through powerful lenses) dressed fleas, Leonardo da Vinci's Last Supper painted on a grain of rice and a sculptured camel passing through the eye of a needle. *Continue on the same road, the C3313, up the valley.*

L'Obrer
(*restaurant,*
Benimantell)

Vicente Ponsoda and his wife Mari Cruz serve wholesome local food including *olleta de blat*, a broth made with beans, bacon, sausage and wheat and *putxero amb pilotes*, meatballs wrapped in cabbage leaves. Homemade desserts include an almond flavoured crème caramel. *Tel 96 588 50 88; closed Fri and Jun 13-Jul 18; price band A/B.*

The C3313 keeps high up the slope, following the contours and passing turnings to Beniardá, Benifato and Abdet: three small, largely unspoilt villages. Above the road hundreds of hill terraces – laid out by the Moors and still irrigated by the same gurgling ditches – go right up to the craggy heights, with only here and there an isolated house. Nearing Confrides which, with its ruined castle on the left of the road, stands at the head of the valley, the terraces thin out and the land

• *Jardín de Santos, Penáguila.*

becomes more wild. After the village the road enters a rocky gorge and climbs towards a high wall of rock into an even bleaker landscape. On the next tight corner is an incongruously-sited bar-restaurant, El Rincón del Olvido, serving Canary Islands dishes; *no phone; closed Mon; price band A.*

Crossing the 966-m pass, Puerto de Ares, you come into a new valley via a series of hairpin bends. *Take the next left turning for Alcoleja and La Vila Joiosa ①. At the T-junction turn right on to the A164 for Penáguila.*

Penáguila   Now just another small town in the hills, Penáguila was once an important country seat. Coats of arms adorn several of the doorways. Parts of the old defensive walls – including one gateway – have been incorporated in later houses. The town is named after the high rocky pinnacle above it – Eagle Rock although sadly there aren't eagles around here any more.

Jardín de Santos, Penáguila

The main reason to come to Penáguila is to see this small but engaging garden set like an oasis amongst the parched hills. It was laid out by a wealthy aristocratic family in the 18thC but is now council property. To visit it contact the mayor, Sr Picó, in advance (*tel 96 551 30 03*). His house is at C/ Virgen del Patrocinio, 46. If you just want a glimpse of the garden you can peer through the gate.

To reach the garden on foot, take the track just before a white bridge which snakes down through the woods and passes between two stone gateposts. This is the formal drive, flanked all the way by cypresses. By car, carry on over the bridge and look out for an unsurfaced track to the left with a 20km/h sign which leads down the hill from a bend about 1 km from the village.

The garden surrounds a rectangular green pond with a waterspout which casts rainbows in the sunshine. Behind the bright blue summer house is an ornamental maze of concentric rectangles of yew and cypress hedges leading to a Cedar of Lebanon. Hidden in a woodland corner is a baroque grotto decorated with stalactites taken from a local cave.

From Penáguila retrace on the road by which you arrived. Turn right on to the A170 for Alcoleja, which gathers around a stone tower with a conical roof: part of the palace of the Marquis of Malferit. Keep straight on through the village. The road now climbs towards the mountains of the Sierra Aitana, under cliffs flushed salmon-pink. After the entrance to the NATO base (the top of the mountain is given over to antennae and two radar domes) you come to a crossroads 1,207 metres up at the Puerto de Tudons. The right turn takes you to a safari park where tigers and elephants roam at an altitude of 1,000 metres. Keep straight on for Sella dropping down in curves with views of the gentler, southern slopes of the Sierra Aitana on left.

Approaching Sella you'll see a lonely pyramid-shaped peak, Puig Campana (1,410 metres) which looks as if a slice has been cut out of it. The slice is called Roldán's Gash. According to legend, the giant Roldán hacked a piece out of the mountain and hurled it into the sea where it became the Island of Benidorm.

Continue on the main road through Sella, which has a castle with a shrine built into it, descending to a landscape carved into ravines of soft red earth. *About 6 km after Sella turn left ② across badlands to the village of Finestrat which sits at the base of Puig Campana.*

Carry straight on through the crossroads beside Bar La Font Casa Miguel. (The left turning takes you past a spring and up the lower slopes of the mountain.)

Finestrat

Park near the crossroads and take the right turning to explore the village. The picturesque square at the heart of this pretty village has

• *The colourful houses of La Vila Joiosa.*

been marred, on one side, by the insensitive construction of a new town hall.

The road from Finestrat crosses a pass and drops towards the coast, providing views of the skyscraper jungle of Benidorm and its wedge-shaped offshore island. *At the T-junction, 9 km from Finestrat, turn left on to the C 3318 towards Callosa. For the next 7 or 8 km there are estates of white villas to either side of the road. The mountain on your left, Ponoch, is known locally as the Sleeping Lion after its shape as seen from this side. La Nucia is entered along an avenue flanked with plane trees. Turn right after the sharp bend, for Altea.*

Polop de la Marina (*detour*)

The picturesquely-located village of Polop de la Marina can be seen from the other side of La Nucia by carrying on along the main road until the end of the built-up area. Only 1 km from La Nucia, Polop has a singular fountain with 221 spouts.

Ca L'Angeles, (*restaurant, Polop*)

There's no written menu in this family-run restaurant in a converted village house on the main road because the dishes depend on the day's shopping, varying from season to season. *Tel 96 587 02 26; closed Tues and Jun 22-Jul 22; price band B.*

From La Nucia the Altea road plunges down a steep hill into a lush valley filled with oranges before heading for the coast through indifferent scenery.

■■■■ ROUTE TWO: 81 KM

From Altea set out along the main road north towards Valencia and turn off for Callosa de Ensarriá through Altea la Vieja (as in Route One). At the mini-roundabout in the centre of Callosa de Ensarriá turn right on to the C3318 for Fuentes del Algar and Tárbena. Immediately after the brick factory take the right turning to Fuentes del Algar (1 km). This pretty waterfall has been developed into a weekend resort with several restaurants specializing in *paella.* Casa Marcos (*tel 96 588 08 68; price band A*) has a swimming pool for a pre-lunch dip. You can also bathe in the chilly water at the bottom of the waterfall.

Continue on the C3318 which follows a valley of medlars, citrus trees and almonds between towering mountains. After Bolulla the road climbs in hairpins giving views back down the valley. Gradually Tárbena, high above, comes into view.

Tárbena

After the expulsion of the Moriscos (Moors who nominally converted to Christianity) in 1609, Tárbena was repopulated with settlers from the Balearic Islands. The local dialect retains an influence of island speech. Another of the Mallorcans' legacies is a particular kind of Tárbena sausage or *botifarra.*

Can Pinet
(*restaurant, Tárbena*)

The Hammer and Sickle flies outside and the Internationale is played at least once a lunchtime, but the politics of the proprietor, the cheery Pinet, are not to be taken too seriously. A veritable folk museum hangs from the beams overhead. *Paella* is the best choice on the menu. *Tel 96 588 41 31; closed Wed; price band A.*

Pension Castell
(*guest house, Castell de Castells*)

This involves a detour: turn left after Tárbena on to the attractive AP1203 for Castell de Castells (11.7 km). Park in the square by the church and ask for directions. Britons Eric and Jan Wright have four cosy bedrooms in this village house popular with mountain walkers. Guestst eat together round the same table. *Tel 96 551 82 54; price band A.*

From Tárbena continue upwards on the road towards Parcent, crossing into another valley carved into innumerable terraced fields. The road loses some of its height, but soon climbs again, curling around wild slopes of dwarf fan palms and rocks towards the wind-swept Coll de Rates (540 metres). After the pass there are splendid views over the Jalón valley, known for its almond trees and vineyards.

Reaching Parcent, turn right ③ on to the A142 for Alcalalí, a village surrounded by budget restaurants popular with the Costa Blanca's Anglo-Saxon residents; among them is Valbon (*tel 96 573 17 71; closed Mon; price band A/B*); and Benarrosa (*tel 96 573 01 06 and 96*

• Peñon de Ifach.

648 20 06; closed Sat; price band A/B).

Turn right by the carpentry factory in Alcalalí for Jalón. Keep on this road, bearing left at the next junction for Jalón. In the *bodega* (on the right as you enter the village) you can buy a range of table and dessert wines, also oak barrels (empty or full). *Turn right before the village centre, for Benissa, and follow the road round to the left.*

Sierra Bernia *(detour)*

Turn right into the narrow street, Calle de la Iglesia, signposted Bernia. This minor road, rough in places, climbs gently through sparsely populated land to the heights of the Sierra Bernia. Some 5 km from Jalón it passes through the hamlet of Maserof, now a vineyard and wine club run by an Englishman. The road levels out and runs below the high peaks. Turn left at the junction for Pinos on the AV1425. You descend steeply, going through the village of Pinos, enjoying stunning views over Calpe and the Peñón de Ifach. Turn right at the T-junction to rejoin the route just before the junction with the N332.

From Jalón, continue straight on past the petrol station for Benissa. The road climbs out of the valley and crosses the motorway to meet the N332. Turn left and continue through Benissa.

Benissa

The older part of town has some immaculate streets. The outsized white neo-classical 'cathedral' treasures a tiny painting, *La Purissima*

Xiqueta, attributed to the 16thC painter Juan de Juanes.
Turn right at the large crossroads at the end of town for Playa and Costa Benissa. The road rises, falls and rises again through vineyards and almond groves. When it levels out, fork right for Calpe. Round a corner you have views of the Peñón de Ifach, a 300-m hunk of rock which rises vertically out of the sea. At the stop sign turn right towards Calpe ④.

Keep to the main road, ignoring the many small lanes leading off into estates of villas. Approaching Calpe the road becomes a dual carriageway, passing the tower blocks of apartments that line the beach. The old salt pans to the right attract a diversity of wildfowl. After the S-bend turn left at the small traffic lights for Peñón de Ifach. Bear left past the Paradero de Ifach hotel and fork left by the Hostal Ancla. Go as far up this road as you can and park by the sign for Parc Natural del Penyal d'Ifach (Peñón de Ifach Nature Reserve). Continue up the unsurfaced road to the reception centre.

Peñón de Ifach

From below, the rock looks unclimbable without ropes and pitons. And so it was until a short tunnel – invisible until you reach it – was built in 1918 to let walkers through to the much gentler slopes on its seaward side. This colossal block of limestone is home to 300 kinds of wild plant including several rare species such as the Calpe carnation. Migrating birds use the Peñón as a landmark. The walk to the top (allow two hours or more), on slopes of juniper and fan palm, sets off to the left of the reception centre. It presents no special difficulty although it helps to have a head for heights. From the exposed and windy summit you can see Ibiza on a clear day.

From the Peñón return to the dual carriageway and turn left towards the town centre. Stay on it as it curves up the hill, avoiding the town centre, to meet the N332. Follow the signs for Alicante under and on to the N332.

Calpe

The old quarter at the top of the hill is a maze of small, stepped streets and squares which have recently been decorated with a series of large pastel-coloured *trompe-l'oeil* murals.

Venta La Chata *(hotel, Calpe)*

Take the N332 north (towards Valencia). The hotel, an old roadside inn with pleasant gardens, is 4 km from Calpe. *Tel 96 583 03 08; price band A.*

Between Calpe and Altea the N332 passes through three short tunnels piercing a great wall of rock, the Morro de Toix, the final buttress of the Sierra Bernia. In between the tunnels comes a bridge over an extremely deep and narrow gorge, the Barranco de Mascarat. You can only get a quick view of it because there is nowhere to stop. On the far side of the gorge there are fine views over the coast taking in the two rocky islets off Altea and the Sierra Helada near Benidorm. The road descends to sea level to enter Altea. This stretch of road can be congested at peak hours during summer.

• *Alconchel, with Miraflores Castle in the background.*

Imagine a countryside as little interfered with as any in western Europe, often described as Spain's 'ecological reserve': plains and *sierra* and above all *dehesa*, a characteristic mix of holm oak trees and cork oaks spread park-like further than the eye can reach. This countryside is blazing hot in summer, a pageant of wildflowers in spring. Red kites endlessly work its open skies; black pigs snuffle under the holm oaks, testing the ground for acorns. Cattle twitch away flies in the pools of shade beneath the trees.

This is Extremadura. In medieval times it was the territory of the old orders of chivalry, first the Knights Templars, and then the Knights of Santiago and Alcántara, both founded locally. Later, it produced an extraordinary proportion of the Conquistadors, those fierce adventurers who seized the even vaster spaces of Latin America.

Extremadura's northern half, the province of Cáceres, though scarcely on the tourist mainline, contains such relatively well-known places of interest as Cáceres itself, Trujillo and the beautiful and important monastery of Guadalupe. This expedition takes you, for contrast, through the even less well-known southern province of Badajoz, taking in a variety of vivid landscapes, a small group of historic towns and a string of villages, not often visited. It is a journey into another Spain.

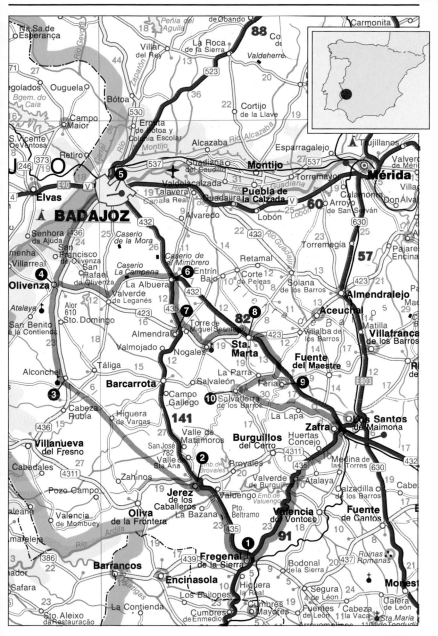

ROUTE: 265 KM **(EXCLUDING DETOURS)**

Zafra
Gentle, if sleepy, its lime-white exteriors contrasting with black wrought-iron window grilles, Zafra is a satisfying balance of the restraint typical of central Spain and the chattier ambience of the south. It is centred around two lovely squares, the Plaza Grande and the Plaza Chica (Big and Little), both arcaded, both charmingly irregular, both wonderful meeting places for late night beers and coffee. At Calle Sevilla 11, you will find a shop selling splendid cowboy boots and chaps, and leather leggings for hunting wild boar in thorny countryside. Zafra's principal building is the nine-towered castle of the Dukes of Feria (see Feria, below). Conquistador Hernán Cortés, born nearby in Medellín, stayed with the duke here before departing for America. Juan de Herrera, architect of the Escorial, is responsible for a cool Renaissance patio within the castle and in later periods dwelling houses and gracious balconies were added to the exterior. The place is now a parador – see below.

Parador Hernán Cortés
(*hotel, Zafra*)
Without doubt, one of the most delightful of the paradors – and that is saying something. Enjoy not only the castle, but also, in hot weather, the swimming pool tucked in beneath the walls. Interesting local menu, especially the mixed *hors d'oeuvres* of tiny oven dishes (*cazuelitas*). *Plaza Corazón María, Zafra, tel 924 55 02 00; price band B/C.*

Leave Zafra south-west in the direction of Fregenal de la Sierra, passing the bullring, on the N435 (Huelva) road – traffic is generally light. The road runs through rolling country with cereal crops, olives and poplars, and with low, softly-moulded *sierra* appearing almost at once to the west. Valverde de Burguillos, in 17 km, is a pleasing village with fountains at most intersections and rose beds lining the streets. "If water was worth as much as oil, we'd all be rich," says the blacksmith ruminatively. The Bar de Justo, close to the church and opposite the blacksmith's, is famous for frogs' legs; evenings, autumn only.

Fregenal de la Sierra
This small town rides a ridge, its castle clearly visible from outside, but almost buried once you arrive at the split-level Plaza de la Constitución in the centre. It stands behind decorative, early 20thC frontages, one applied to the church that leans against the castle walls and another to the market actually within the castle. There is a bullring inside the castle, too, a remarkable place to which Senóra Lola keeps the key. Anyone will help you find her. One of Spain's greatest gipsy festivals is held here each October.

España,
(*restaurant, Fregenal*)
Food tends to the simple in the small settlements of southern Extremadura and most restaurants exist to supply a basic need, not to provide a dining experience. That said, the España is perfectly acceptable. *Plaza de la Constitución; tel. 924 70 01 24; price band A.*

• *The imposing Parador Hernán Cortés, Zafra.*

① *Return to the N435 and back-track to the eastern side of town. Here, turn left and north, for Jerez de los Caballeros.* Give or take a few large fig trees, the countryside soon turns into *debesa*. Coming down finally through hills to a wide valley, you see Jerez de los Caballeros opposite, looking like an Andalucian White Town with the addition of Baroque church towers and the southern walls of a great Templar castle.

Jerez de los Caballeros   The powerful and secretive Knights Templars of Jerez de los Caballeros became victims of a combined royal and papal plot in 1312. Refusing to surrender, the Templars held out in the castle. Finally defeated, they were hanged and their bodies exhibited on the walls of the Bloody Tower, the Torre Sangrienta. This is on the outer wall, seen to your left as you drive up the last hill into town and easily reached on foot (via the Town Hall gardens, the Town Hall itself being housed in the castle). Jerez is an up-and-down place of narrow streets, with arched gateways and sedate mansions. Its finest architectural feature is the series of amazingly extravagant Baroque church towers, the best being the highest on the hill – San Bartolomé, with gleaming blue ceramic decorations. Its Holy Week processions are famous in western Spain.

La Ermita
(bar, Jerez)   Occupying a 17thC Baroque chapel of the former Hermitage in Calle

• *Baroque church tower, Jerez de los Caballeros.*

Dr Benitez s/n, La Ermita serves Extremaduran *tapas* – *chorizo*, pig's ear and so forth – as well as meals. Scruffily atmospheric.

Oasis
(restaurant, Jerez)

A *hostal* and restaurant above the church of San Bartolomé – where local shopkeepers, the vet and the bank manager eat not badly at all in welcome air-conditioning. *Calle el Campo 18; tel. 924 73 12 44; price band A/B..*

Los Templarios
(hotel, Jerez)

You will find it at the town's edge on the (tiny) main road leading out through the top of the town, west to Villanueva de los Fresnos. A large, brand-new building which still stands somewhat gaunt, but offering

• *Bullring within the castle at Fregenal de la Sierra, venue for a famous gypsy festival.*

creature comforts and fine views, especially from its swimming pool. *Carretera de Villanueva s/n; tel 924 73 16 36; price band B/C.*

② *Continue another 6 km on the Villanueva road, then turn right as signposted for Higuera de Vargas.* You now experience deeply remote, classic *dehesa* country, with dirt roads departing through the trees towards unseen ranches or *fincas* with their white-washed stone gateposts. Higuera de Vargas is a desolate seeming little place, not worth turning into. *Continue on flatter and more open ground to Alconchel, 47 km from Jerez, turning right on to the C436 for the final approach.*

Alconchel   Miraflores Castle, another Templar stronghold, stands wonderfully irregular on a cone of mountain, with split-level outer walls surrounding a stout keep, high above the quiet little town of Alconchel and completely out of scale in its grandeur. You may well see charcoal burners at work in the vicinity, practising an ancient trade now largely devoted to fuelling the barbecue business. They build large piles of timber, arranged like a monk's tonsure, then cover the pile with earth and burn away.

③ *Continue 21 km north along the C436, through open countryside,* sierra *always in view, to* ④ *Olivenza.*

Olivenza   A small white town of beauty and charm, completely Portuguese in

• *The Alameda, in the Portuguese-influenced town, Olivenza.*

style. Indeed it always was Portuguese until Manuel Godoy, the local guards officer who became lover to the queen and Spain's prime minister at the age of 25, won it for his country at the peace which concluded the War of the Oranges in 1801.

It has a splendidly pugnacious castle (long walk up internal ramps rewarded by fine views), with a museum of local life and crafts in the outbuildings below (open summer, 11-2, 7-9; Sat and Sun 12-2). Olivenza's major monument, however, is the delightful church of La Magdalena, built in the Portuguese Manuelline Gothic style, with twisted barley sugar columns and a feast of Portuguese tiles (usually open mornings). There are more fine tiles in the chapel of the Misercordia, open 10-2. The castle church will probably be shut for restoration.

Don't miss the façade and clock tower of the late 15thC Casas Consistoriales in the Plaza de la Constitución; be sure, too, just to spend some time strolling about, absorbing the atmosphere. You may catch some pleasant cooking smells: Olivenza is home of *tecula mecula,* a dessert made with almonds and pork lard (*tocino*), also of of *piñonate,* a pastry loaded with cinnamon and honey, and rich in olive oil.

If you feel hungry, Dosca is a pleasant restaurant, serving Extremaduran and Spanish dishes. *Plaza de la Constitución 15; tel 924*

49 10 65; price band A.

A reasonably priced place to stay in, adequate comfort but no high living, is the Hotel Heredero on the northern exit from Olivenza. *Carretera de Badajoz s/n; tel. 49 08 35; price band B.*

Badajoz
(55-km detour)

Should you want a pause from the rural experience, carry on 27 km north from Olivenza to Badajoz ⑤, the provincial capital.

Badajoz has had a bad press through the ages. As a frontier town on the Portuguese border, it was often laid waste. In the Civil War it was the scene of a massacre when some hundreds of leftists were rounded up and shot in the bullring. Its most historic district, largely Moorish in architecture, up around the Plaza Alta, is poor and threatening and best avoided. Yet despite, or even because of all this, Badajoz has a definite, almost outcast appeal. Its curious old cathedral has a cloister jam-packed with Arab-style tiles and possesses paintings by the locally-born Mannerist painter, Luis Morales, known as El Divino. There are pleasant little 19thC streets and a fine river bank along the Guadiana, with a handsome bridge by Juan Herrera and a triumphal entry gate.

For accommodation, try the four-star Gran Hotel Zurbarán, named for Extremadura's other great painter. It is modern-ish and fairly smart. Lovely river views, especially at sunset. *Paseo de Castelar s/n; tel 924 22 37 41.*

Return to Olivenza ④. Your route back to Zafra now makes a double zig-zag through a series of Extremaduran villages, with sharply differing histories, settings and even local products.

From Olivenza, on the Badajoz side of town, head east following signs for Valverde de Leganés. Don't bother to enter the village, but immediately afterwards take the Badajoz road left past the petrol station and then sharp right, just before the cemetery (a typically high white-walled enclosure with coffin niches in the walls) for La Albuera.

On entering La Albuera, ⑥ turn right along the N432 in the direction of Zafra. Of several eating places here, try the garishly decorated Lope, on the right. *Tel 924 48 00 87; price band A.*

Opposite Lope, down Avenida General Castaños, you'll find a handsome little monument celebrating one of the Peninsular War's great victories. At the Battle of La Albuera, May 16, 1811, British, Portuguese and Spanish troops, commanded by Generals Castaños, Beresford and Blake, trounced the French under Marshal Soult as he advanced to raise the siege of Badajoz.

Continue through La Albuera on the N432 and, on the edge of the village, angle right on the N435 in the direction, once again, of Jerez de los Caballeros. After 13 km pull off right to explore the charming white village of Almendral ⑦. Leave the village eastwards on a road unsignposted at time of going to press, crossing the main road by the Talleres Hermanos Moreno, a large repairs garage. Continue to Nogales, 8 km from Almendral.

• *Feria, viewed from the castle.*

The *sierra* now runs along south of the road, presenting a horizon both sinuous and lumpy. In front, the castle of Nogales rises neat as a pin on a cone of hill, reminiscent of Alconchel, while yet another castle-on-a-cone, later to be revealed as that of Feria, home of the dukes, briefly appears in the distance then disappears again.

In Nogales it is worth turning off and climbing through the village to the castle, though it feels somewhat abandoned when you get there. Returning to the main road, carry on 11 km, through a district of vines, black pig-farming and spendid fig orchards, with the earth now turning pimiento red, to ⑧ Santa Marta.

You have now entered the Tierra de Barros, or Land of Mud, an increasingly important wine-growing district, pancake-flat in parts and offering little to the eye. Santa Marta, despite its dispiriting looks, has a *bodega* where local Blasón del Turra wines may be tasted and bought. Of several restaurants (you have once again rejoined the N432 to Zafra) Kika must be clear favourite, serving excellent chick peas with *chorizo* and blood sausage. There's an old yellow tram car perched outside, bearing the legend *Extremadura una y universal*: On the main road, the *Teniente Coronel Segui*, at no. 21; tel. 924 690 527; price band A/B.

Now continue 14 km along the N432, then turn right, climbing in 4 km to Feria ⑨*,* which has one of the most notable of all the castles on the journey. The walls and keep of Feria are impressive enough: you may well find the keep unlocked (beware holes in the floors if you decide to climb up). But the real excitement is the position – the sense of an eagle's eyrie, with views far out over the Tierra de Barros, its white towns floating like islands on a lake. Behind lies the *sierra,* smooth in outline, knobbly in vegetation. Below, the white village of Feria rises up and up along the road, its houses ascending in stiff little steps. Skip Nogales, skip Alconchel, but don't miss the castle at Feria.

It would be possible to return from here to the main road and uneventfully to cruise the final 17 km to Zafra. However, if you have the energy, it is even more of a pleasure to strike into the low-altitude but passably rugged *sierra, taking the road to La Parra as you descend from Feria, and from La Parra to Salvatierra de los Barros.* ⑩ This last is a village almost entirely dedicated to the production of earthenware, sometimes plain, but often decorated with incised floral patterns. Some is a lustrous reddish-brown, while other pots are black, creating a curious effect.

From here, it is a short but beautiful drive through *sierra* and *dehesa* to Zafra, (a total of 43 km from Feria). The scenery is almost African. Cistus and wild lavender flower profusely in spring. In summer the dry stream beds are awash with the pink of oleander. Re-enter Zafra through a medieval gate.

• *The olive groves of Jaén.*

The thickly-forested limestone ridges and deep, steep-sided valleys of the Sierra de Cazorla form the heart of Spain's largest nature reserve. These mountains, reaching 2,107 metres, are rich in rare plants and animals. Rarest of the rare – down to a single pair – is the lammergeier, known as 'the bone smasher' in Spanish because of its habit of breaking bones against rocks to suck out the marrow.

This haven used to be a shooting gallery: Franco was once among the bands of hunters and fishermen attracted by Cazorla's non-protected species, especially deer, mouflon, wild boar and Spanish ibex. A good time to visit the area is in September when you can hear stags baying threats at each other.

On both these routes you are never far from the Guadalquivir, one of Spain's most important rivers, which rises in the Sierra de Cazorla and flows across Andalucia to Seville. The first route follows the nascent Guadalquivir through the centre of the reserve and out of it by means of a gorge. Route Two offers an absorbing contrast to the wildlife, crossing the province of Jaén's vast olive groves to visit Ubeda and Baeza, two noble towns packed with Renaissance architecture.

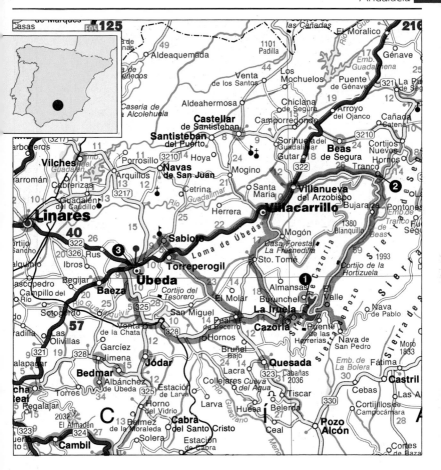

ROUTE ONE: 130 KM

Cazorla Clinging to a steep slope beneath the rocky ridge of Los Halcones (`the Falcons'), Cazorla looks out over an undiluted view of olive groves. Park in the Plaza de la Constitución and walk down Calle Doctor Muñoz to the Plaza de la Corredera, the centre of the town. Continue in the same direction into the old part of town: a pretty labyrinth of narrow streets which emerges on the Plaza de Santa María with its Renaissance fountain and the atmospheric shell of the church of Santa María. Close by the square castle looms impressively. On the night of May 14, during the fiesta honouring Cazorla's patron saint, the old

• *Castillo de Cazorla.*

streets of the town are illuminated by lamps made by filling snail shells with oil.

Confusingly, there are four tourist information offices in the town – two of them run by private companies offering four-wheel drive tours of restricted areas of the nature reserve.

Villa Turística (*hotel, Cazorla*)

More like an exclusive housing estate than a hotel, the Villa Turística comprises self-contained apartments arranged on a steep hillside looking across the valley at Cazorla's picturesque old quarter and the castle. You can choose self-catering (at an extra charge) or eat in the hotel's average but inexpensive restaurant. *Tel 953 71 01 00; Ladera de San Isicio; price band A.*

From the Plaza de la Constitución take the road to the Sierra. Leaving the town, you pass beneath La Iruela. Park in the small car park on the right just before the Hotel Sierra de Cazorla. From here a steep staircase ascends to the magnificent ruins of La Iruela's Templar castle, precariously perched above a cliff.

In Burunchel, 5 km from Cazorla, you pass through a nature reserve checkpoint where a guard takes your car number. The road zig-zags up through mixed woodland to a pass, the Puerto de las Palomas, from which there are views over interminable hills of olives in one direction and the deep valleys and ridges of the Sierra to the other.

Dropping down into a thickly wooded valley you come to ① *the reserve's principal junction, El Empalme del Valle. Turn left here: down the valley towards Torre del Vinagre and El Tranco.*

Parador El Adelantado
(hotel, Cazorla)

To find it, carry straight on at El Empalme and turn right at the next junction after 2.5 km. This modern hotel in a superb mountain forest setting is a useful base for walks. The building lacks intrinsic charm and is unimaginatively furnished, but it offers the predictable Parador standard of catering and service. *Tel 953 72 10 75; price band B.*

Source of the Guadalquivir
(38-km detour)

Carry on past the Parador turn off. In half a kilometre take the next right turn. The 15thC bridge, Puente de las Herrerías, is said to have been built in a single night to allow Queen Isabel and her Christian forces to proceed swiftly to the conquest of Moorish Granada. An unsurfaced road continues 11 km to the source of the Guadalquivir, a spring surrounded by rocks.

From El Empalme, the road along the valley descends through thick woods. After about 4 km you cross the fledgling Guadalquivir, still no more than a stream. Levelling out, the valley floor becomes wide enough to accommodate pastures as well as hotels and holiday homes. The next time you cross the Guadalquivir its volume has noticeably increased.

Noguera de la Sierpe
(hotel/restaurant, Coto Ríos)

This claret-coloured hotel between the road and the river is filled with the owner's hunting trophies from her African safaris. Animal lovers may feel uneasy with the antler lamp brackets and clothes pegs made from hooves. The restaurant serves trout and game. *Tel 953 72 17 09; price band B.*

Torre del Vinagre

The nature reserve's reception centre has illuminated displays on the local wildlife, and the inevitable souvenir shop. Next door is a hunting museum sparsely decorated with horns, weapons and stuffed specimens of the major game species. In theory, the botanical garden across the road presents indigenous species according to the height to which they grow in the wild; in practice it's a somewhat disorganized mixture of native and imported plants. The gardener, however, is a cheery old soul with time to talk to plant lovers.

Borosa Fish Farm
(3-km detour)

A turning opposite the Torre del Vinagre takes you to a trout hatchery beside the river where large, open tanks fizz with life. An unsurfaced road continues up the picturesque Borosa valley.

From Torre del Vinagre continue down the Guadalquivir valley for a further 11 km until you come to the Bar El Parque and signs for Parque Cinegético (Hunting Reserve). Park behind the bar.

Parque Cinegético del Collado del Almendral

Broad paths lead up the hill through the woods to three observation platforms overlooking an enclosure where deer and mouflon roam in protected liberty. The nearest observatory is 650 metres from the car park, the furthest 900 metres. Behind the enclosure is El Tranco reservoir or at least, in dry years, the bed of it. In late September/early October male deer can often be seen and heard baying threats at each other across this open space. The best times to visit Collado del Almendral are midday and 6pm when the animals are fed. At other times you can also see many species of birds flying over the bed of the reservoir and hopping between the trees. If you want to stretch your legs some more, there's a 1.5-km walk back to the car park over the hill.

The road continues through the trees beside the reservoir. Reaching El Tranco you pass through another checkpoint to leave the reserve. Cross the dam and ② turn left towards Villanueva del Arzobispo.

Segura de la Sierra *(58-km detour)*

If you have time to continue exploring the reserve, keep straight on beside the lake in El Tranco to see the more open, less forested northern part. Turn right after Cortijos Nuevos to reach Segura de la Sierra, a dramatically sited village huddling below a restored castle on the summit of a 1,113-metre peak.

The next few kilometres are through the deep tree-filled gorge of the Guadalquivir with great reddish cliffs rising above it. Gradually the slopes become less severe, admitting olive groves. The road rises out of the gorge on to rolling farmland. Ahead, Iznatoraf sits on the summit of a prominent hill.

Turn left on to the main road (N322) and take the next right turning to Iznatoraf. Park in the main square outside the church.

Iznatoraf

There are all-round views from the balconies fringing the town centre. To the south you can see Cazorla and La Iruela clinging to the hillside;

• *The castle at Segura de la Sierra.*

to the south-west is Sabiote, another ancient hill top town (see Route Two). Some streets are crossed by arches. Older houses have coats of arms carved in stone above their doorways. One house behind the church has embedded columns and carved capitals in its façade, and a face carved under the eaves.

Return to the main road and turn right, carrying on to Villacarrillo. Turn off left for Mogón and Santo Tomé. Turn right after the petrol station towards the town centre and turn left shortly, again for Mogón and Santo Tomé.

Villacarillo   Not one of the most interesting places in the area, but there is a town hall with an 18thC façade and a church, La Asunción, which is attributed to Jaén's acclaimed Renaissance architect, Vandelvira.

The return route to Cazorla crosses agricultural land, by-passes the undistinguished town of Mogón and crosses the Guadalquivir to reach Santo Tomé. Some historians claim that Mogón was mentioned by Ptolemy in the 2ndC BC as Mentesa Oretana. Turn left in the town for Cazorla.

ROUTE TWO: 125 KM

• *The walls and gate of Sabiote castle.*

Leave Cazorla on the road to Peal de Becerro (the C328). Keep straight on through Peal de Becerro in the direction of Ubeda. The two medieval towers dominating its skyline are best admired from a distance.

Toya Iberian Tomb
(12-km detour)

Collect the keys for this subterranean hill-top burial chamber from Peal de Becerro town hall. Turn sharp left for Toya at the crossroads at the end of the town. In 5 km the tomb is signposted; you have to continue another 1 km on unsurfaced track.

To follow the main route, keep straight on at the crossroads in Peal de Becerro for Ubeda and Torreperogil.

Puente de la Cerrada Reservoir

After 9 km you cross a small dam, Puente de la Cerrada, holding back the waters of the Guadalquivir to irrigate the dry land around. It has been declared a nature reserve in order to protect such species as the purple gallinule and bar- and black-tailed godwits.

From here the road winds upwards for 13 km through olive groves to Torreperogil.

Torreperogil

An almost unknown wine-producing town, Torreperogil's only other merit is the church of Santa María, a mixture of Gothic and Renaissance.

• Chapel of San
Salvador,
Ubeda.

*Turn right at the T-junction in Torreperogil towards Albacete. When you
reach the main road, the N322, turn left towards Ubeda. In 1 km turn right
on to the J6011 for Sabiote.*

Sabiote   Protected by a scarp slope to the north-east, Sabiote has well-
preserved Arab ramparts and a thick-walled medieval castle. Despite its
attractive situation and its evident history, the town is ignored by most
tourists, who don't stray out of Ubeda. As a result it is a refreshingly
unassuming place. Washing is hung out in the square in front of the
castle. Its streets of white houses are interspersed with mansions
bearing carved portals and coats of arms. Park at the end of the

• *Stone window detail of Baeza's cathedral.*

pedestrianised street, Gallego Diaz, and walk down Calle del Canónigo Utrera to the outskirts of the town from which there are views across the plain. From here it is a short walk past the old walls to the castle.

Take the road down to Ubeda. When you get to the main road turn right on to it and left at the next traffic lights for Centro Ciudad. Follow the purple signs for Conjunto Histórico-Artístico and you should find your way into the Plaza del Primero de Mayo. There may be parking spaces here. You can get even closer to the sights if you continue to the Plaza del Ayuntamiento and the Plaza Vázquez de Molina (the monumental square at the centre of the old city) where there is a car park outside the Parador.

Ubeda

This grand showcase of Spanish Renaissance architecture is largely the work of architect Andrés de Vandelvira (1509-75) under the patronage of two ambitous courtiers, Francisco de los Cobos and Juan Vázquez de Molina. The most impressive buildings surround the Plaza Vázquez de Molina. Two of the former palaces on the square have been put to new uses: the Dean of Malaga's residence, surrounding a delightful patio, has become a parador (tel 953 75 03 45); and the Palacio de las Cadenas is now the town hall. At one end of the square stands the Sacred Chapel of St Salvador with its decorated façade and over-ornate interior. One of Valdevira's finest works, the Hospital de

Santiago (under restoration), is on the outskirts near the bullring.

Palacio de la Rambla
(hotel, Ubeda)
Where better to stay in Ubeda than in the home of the Marquesa de la Rambla whose palace is one of Ubeda's listed sights? The patio is attributed to Vandelvira and the rooms are furnished with heirlooms. Guests have included King Alfonso XIII. *Tel 953 75 01 96; price band C.*

To leave the centre of Ubeda, follow the signs for Todas Direcciones and then Jaén, which will bring you on to the main road, the N321. After 8 km you enter Baeza. Follow the signs for Barrio Monumental until you reach the Plaza del Populo; park nearby.

Baeza
The centre of Baeza, like Ubeda, is littered with monuments. Begin your tour in the small square off the bottom of the Plaza del Populo. The Fountain of the Lions, in the middle of the square, was built with blocks of stone taken from the Roman town of Castulo. Looking on to it are two monumental gateways, side by side; also two handsome buildings: the former abbatoir (in use until the 1960s); and what is now the tourist office. Head up the hill and you reach the cathedral, remodelled in the 16thC but including some of its earlier Gothic elements. In front of it is a quaint triumphal-arched fountain. The seminary opposite the cathedral is rudely adorned with fading red scrawl. Traditionally, the graduates of Baeza's former university – it closed in the 19thC – signed their names on this wall in bull's blood. On the way back down the hill you pass the best of Baeza's noble homes, the Jabalquinto Palace with its Isabelline façade studded with carved stone diamonds.

R Juanito
(restaurant, Baeza)
This celebrated family-run restaurant (Campsa-recommended) has a humble location next to a petrol station on the Ubeda road. Olive oil is a major feature of the cooking and various brands of olive oil are on sale in the dining-room. Before you buy a bottle you can sample 20 or more different types from all over Spain from a trolley brought to your table. In the hallway are photographs of the bullfighters, politicians and other dignitaries who have eaten here – among them the King of Spain. *Tel 953 74 00 40; closed Sun and Mon evening; price band B.*

Return along the main road towards Ubeda but before the town turn right ③ at the junction beside the petrol station for Iznallof and Jódar on the C325. After crossing the River Guadalquivir turn left for Cazorla and Peal de Becerro on the C328. The road crosses over the Linares-Almería railway line three times and then once under it. Turn left for Cazorla and Peal de Becerro through rolling fields of cereals and olives, leaving Hornos on a hill to the right. Reaching Peal, turn right through the town towards Cazorla.

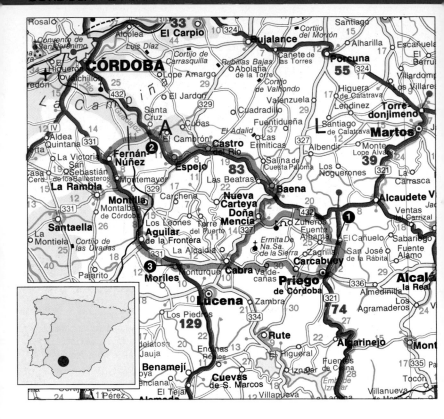

These two loops look at quite distinct parts of the province of Córdoba, an area wholly overlooked by tourists on whistle-stop tours between the Great Mosque at Córdoba and the Alhambra in Granada.

The first circuit visits the sparsely vegetated but nonetheless attractive hills of the Sierra Subbética, taking in Priego de Córdoba, renowned for its Baroque architecture, and ending with Zuheros, one of the prettiest villages in Andalucia.

The second loop tours La Campiña, an open country of olive trees, vineyards and cereals. The high point here is a visit to the wine cellars of Montilla, Spain's alternative sherry capital, from which you may well return laden with bottles.

Tourism is only just beginning to find its way to these parts and the locals living in the towns of Córdoba's backroads aren't

• Zuheros, with the castle behind.

much used to foreigners. You may even surprise them by asking for directions to some local sight. Many of the monuments along the way are privately owned, neglected or else under restoration; but patience and persistence in finding such places will be repaid by the satisfaction of seeing things not mentioned in most of the standard guidebooks on Spain.

ROUTE ONE: 113 KM

Baena

With its rich soil and abundant water, an old Roman settlement on this site was transformed into the prosperous Muslim town of Bayyana, living off vineyards and olive groves. Today, Baena's olive oil is recognized as among the best in Spain and has its own *denominación de origen*.

Sadly the historic part of town, La Almedina, at the top of the hill, has been neglected. Part of the once-important Moorish fortress has been turned into a bar and the rest left in ruins. The Gothic church of Santa María, with its Isabelline portal, is however under restoration (but most of its art treasures went up in flames during the Civil War). Next to the church is the 16thC Convent of Madre de Dios with a curious look-out balcony, the Arco de la Villa, bridging the street. At Christmas and Easter the nuns sell home-made cakes through a hatch. You will be greeted with the salutation "*Ave María Purísima*" ("Hail the pure Virgin") from a disembodied voice behind a turntable to which you are expected to reply "*Sin pecado concebida*" ("Conceived without sin") before placing your order.

There are two Moorish gateways on the edge of the old town. During Easter Week celebrations in Baena two teams of richly-dressed drummers compete to see who can beat the fastest.

Leave Baena on the N432 in the direction of Granada but turn off by the petrol station at the end of town on to the C321 for Cabra.

El Zambudio *Take the left turning for Zuheros and after 2.5 km turn right as signposted.*
(*hotel, Baena*) You will find a large house with a curving verandah and a kidney-shaped swimming pool sunk into a shady lawn. The Zambudio is little known except by the travelling salesmen who make up most of its guests. Comfortable, almost luxurious, it is surprisingly economical. *Tel 957 670837; price band A/B.*

The road climbs above Baena with views of the hill-top fortifications, then winds round slopes of olive groves to Doña Mencía, a wine-producing town with a ruined castle. In another 14 km, after crossing and re-crossing an abandoned railway line several times, you enter Cabra through a modern monumental gateway. Carry straight on through the modern part of town and cross the junction with traffic

• *The battlements, Cabra castle.*

lights to reach the old quarter, or *barrio viejo.*

Cabra

Park in the square beside the church of La Asunción y Angeles and have a stroll in the narrow streets behind it which are lined with whitewashed houses. Old ramparts fringe the square, but the castle is occupied by a religious order. A quarry near Cabra supplied much of the marble for the great mosque at Córdoba and there's plenty of it inside the Baroque interior of La Asunción y Angeles. Much more discreet is the church of San Juan Bautista which dates from the 7thC, making it one of the oldest in Andalucia.

Mesón del Vizconde
(*restaurant, Cabra*)

The Mediterranean coast may seem a world away from Cabra, but this family-run restaurant in the town centre serves excellent fish and seafood cooked in the best local olive oil. *Tel 957 52 17 02; closed Tues; price band B.*

From the centre of Cabra take the road for Priego de Córdoba. After 2 km you pass the Fuente del Río gardens, busy at weekends but peaceful for picnics on weekdays. Across the road is the municipal swimming pool. Turn left shortly on to the C336 which climbs quickly into the hills.

Nuestra Señora de la Sierra

Turn left on to the little road signposted for Ermita de Nuestra Señora de la Sierra which winds up bare, rocky slopes to the wooded summit of el Picacho (1,223 metres). The shrine to Our Lady of the Mountain was founded in the 13thC. In June it is the focus of a pilgrimage from Cabra.

• The diminutive cliff-top castle at Zuheros.

This is supposedly the geographical centre of Andalucia; certainly there are tremendous views in all directions. To the south is another conical peak topped with a shrine: that of Nuestra Señora de Araceli, near Lucena.

Return down the lane and turn left on to the main road towards Priego de Córdoba passing, on your right, the hill-top town and castle of Carcabuey. When you reach Priego follow the signs for centro ciudad *and park as near to the central square, Plaza Constitución, as you can.*

Priego de Córdoba

In the 17th and 18thC Priego had a thriving silk and textile industry. The wealth from this helped fill the town with an extraordinary collection of Baroque architecture. The churches of La Asunción (in particular the Sagrario chapel) and La Aurora are especially noted for their extravagant interiors. Priego's best-known Baroque monument is a fountain at the end of Calle Río, La Fuente del Rey, in which water pours from 139 spouts into three basins adorned with sculptures. The prettiest part of Priego is much older. The Barrio de la Villa, the former Moorish quarter, is a warren of tapering streets, lined with white houses leaning towards each other, kept scrupulously clean by its proud inhabitants. On one side La Villa is bordered by the cliff-top Paseo del Adarve from which there are views over the surrounding countryside. Try and visit Priego on a Saturday night when, at midnight,

• La Fuente del Rey, Priego de Córdoba.

a band of minstrels clad in black and holding lanterns walks the streets singing songs of praise to the Virgin Mary.

To leave the town, follow the signs for Jaén and Baena, turning left off the Avenida Granada and crossing Priego's by-pass. Once on the Jaén road proper you enter a short gorge, Las Angosturas. After El Cañuelo turn off left ① on to the narrow road for Fuente Alhama and Luque, slipping down into the valley around numerous curves. Bear left at the next junction and turn right up the hill at the subsequent T-junction towards Luque. Keep on this road which climbs out of the valley and around the hillside giving views of the farmland to the north. Ignore the left turning to Luque on an

• *Palace of the Dukes, Fernán Nuñez.*

unsurfaced road unless you are feeling adventurous. The surfaced road takes a more indirect route, dropping down to meet the main Córdoba-Granada road, the N432. Turn left on to it. In a few kilometres, after Estación de Luque, turn off left for Luque, a white town spilling down from a saddle and watched over by a castle, isolated on a rocky hill. Continue around the hillside to Zuheros.

Zuheros   If there is one village in Andalucia worth lingering in, this is it: a tight cluster of winding, immaculately-kept streets of white houses and red pantiled roofs. The diminutive castle hanging over a cliff and overshadowing the main square is being restored but is still a must to explore. Ask for the keys from the town hall.

Cueva de   *Signposted from the Luque road at the entrance to Zuheros.* These caves
los   on top of a hill overlooking the town were discovered in 1897 but not
Murciélagos explored for another 40 years. The various corridors and chambers have formations of stalactites and stalagmites but more interesting are the unique, diagramatic Neolithic paintings of goats daubed on some of the walls. Finds in the caves suggest that they were inhabited as long ago as 4,300 BC. A skeleton lies in one of the deepest chambers. Even if the caves are closed, it's still worth the drive for the magnificent views from the car park at the entrance. There is a ticket and information office on the right of the road just above the town. *Open Sat, Sun and*

holidays 10 am-12 midday and 4-6 pm (spring) or 6-8 pm (summer). Only 150 visitors are allowed in each day and it is best to book in advance (tel. 957 694514).

Zuhayra
(hotel, Zuheros)

On the road down from the church. A large building in keeping with the predominating village style, the Zuhayra is a simple place – somewhat Spartan furnishings – but adequate for enjoying the peace of Zuheros. *Tel 957 694 624; price band A.*

Take the steep street down past the Hotel Zuhayra and cross over the road at the bottom of the slope for Baena. On the way you pass (without realizing it) the hamlet of Marbella, as inconspicuous as its Costa del Sol namesake is brash, and a left turning to Hotel El Zambudio. You emerge on the Cabra road just outside Baena. Turn right and either take a left turning up the hill towards the town centre or continue to the main road and turn left there.

▬▬▬▬ ROUTE TWO: 137 KM

Leave Baena on the main road (N432) in the direction of Córdoba, which cuts across the unbounded olive groves and cereal fields of La Campiña, passing the occasional palatial farmstead, or cortijo.

Castro del Río

While working as a tax-collector, Cervantes was imprisoned for a week in 1592 in the basement of the town hall, allegedly for overstepping his duties. Don't bother to enter the town, where there is little to see, but keep on the N432 towards Córdoba.

Espejo

The Mudéjar castle of the Dukes of Osuna, one of the great aristocratic families of Andalucia, dominates the skyline from all points in the surrounding country. The castle is private: the best you can do is peer through its gate and stroll round its walls. To get there, drive up the hill to the town hall and market and continue upwards on a straight, narrow street until you reach a steeply sloping car-park on your right. The castle is a few paces further on.

Continue on the N432 for a further 9 km. Before the bridge ② over the River Guadajoz turn left on to the lane signposted for Fernán Nuñez.

Fernán Nuñez

Entering the town you will see the conspicuous claret coloured palace of the Dukes of Fernán Nuñez, built in the 1780s. Park in the courtyard surrounded by matching coloured buildings, one of which is the town hall. You'll be among the first tourists to come looking for this attraction-to-be which is not yet open to the public. Already in an advanced state of disrepair, the palace was handed over to the town council by the present Duke when he found that he could no longer afford its upkeep. Unfortunately, he took most of his art collection with him to Madrid. If you ask in the town hall, someone may show you

• *Octagonal square, Aguilar de la Frontera.*

around the palace, which has a dome over its staircase and various salons with delicately painted ceilings. The formal terraced garden behind has been fully restored to its original condition.

Continue through the town and, on the other side, turn left on to the N331 in the direction of Antequera.

Montemayor The 14thC castle of the Dukes of Frías is closed to the public but the square and streets nearby are pretty and worth a stroll.

After another few kilometres on the main road, turn off on to the C329 for Montilla, passing Las Camachas restaurant on your right. Turn left into the town centre.

Las Camachas (*restaurant, Montilla*) It may look like an unattractive road-side bar, but Las Camachas is the place to eat at in Montilla. As well as *à la carte* delicacies such as *rabo de toro* (bull's tail) and *tocino de cielo*, (a dessert), there is a cheaper *menú del día*. Bottles of local wine are on sale at the bar. *Tel 957 65 00 04; price band A/B.*

Montilla Anyone in town will tell you that Montilla's finos (dry white wines) are better than sherry; and that the fierce Cordoban sunshine makes them so strong that they don't need to be fortified with extra alcohol. If the

Montilla-Moriles *denominación de origen* isn't as internationally famous as that of Jerez de la Frontera, then maybe that is a good reason to try the wines here; they are generally considered to be good value. Amontillado – the term describing a type of pale dry sherry – is derived from Montilla.

Most of the *bodegas* (wineries) will show you around their cellars and let you try their produce. The largest is Alvear, which also claims to be the oldest *bodega* in Spain. They prefer you to book a visit in advance (tel 957 65 01 00).

If you can break away from the wine-tasting, at the far end of town from Bodegas Alvear are two interesting buildings. The Mudéjar convent of Santa Clara, next to an arched gateway over the street, is concealed behind a large, unmarked but open door. You can step into the rustic courtyard and have a look at the church's carved portal. Up the hill, in a street to the right, is the so-called Casa del Inca, formerly the home of Garcilaso de la Vega, historian of the Incas. It is now a library.

Retrace to the N331 and turn left, again heading south for Antequera.

Don Gonzalo
(hotel, Montilla)
To the right of the N331. Despite being a modern roadside complex including a discothèque, the 29-room Don Gonzalo has more than a touch of style and elegance in its interior decoration. You will welcome the swimming pool if you are touring in mid summer. *Tel 957 65 0658; price band B.*

Aguilar
It can be tricky to work your way through Aguilar's complicated street plan to the centre, but if you manage you'll find a handsome 19thC octagonal square, the Plaza de San José.

Laguna de Zonar
(detour)
Immediately after Aguilar, turn left towards Puente Genil on the C329. In 5 km you will come to the information centre of the Lagunas de Córdoba Nature Reserve located on the shore of the Laguna de Zonar. This is the largest of six little-known salt water lakes which are visited in winter by waterfowl. The most noteworthy species is the white-headed duck (with a bright blue bill), a rarity in Europe.

Return along the C329 and turn right back on to the N 331. After by-passing Monturque, turn left ③ on to the C336 to Cabra.

Moriles
(detour)
Turn off right after Aguilar. Wine enthusiasts may want to visit Montilla's smaller partner in the Montilla-Moriles *denominación de origen* where they will find more *bodegas. Take the road through Monturque to rejoin the route.*

Reaching Cabra, follow the signs for Doña Mencía, Baena and Córdoba. A ring road leads you around the town, passing beside a park, to reach the C327. Turn right on to it and return north to Baena via Doña Mencía.

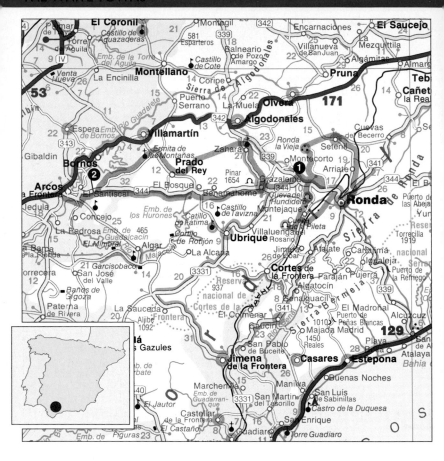

The brilliantly whitewashed town (or village) of tapering streets, windows coyly hidden behind full-length iron grilles, is a trademark of southern Spain. You'll find the archetypal Andalucian White Towns dotting the steep slopes of the mountains which bulge out behind Gibraltar, between the Mediterranean and the Atlantic; these routes connect the two largest and most spectacularly sited, Ronda and Arcos de la Frontera.

Many place names in these parts are suffixed 'de La Frontera', recalling the three centuries during which the White Towns policed the boundary between Christian and Moslem Spain. The

• Puente Nuevo, Ronda.

Christians eventually took the territory but the Moorish influence lives on in the towns' labyrinthine layouts, following the contours of the hills. The uncompromising geography of this area later made it a safe haunt for bandits and smugglers.

The area is not only rich in man-made beauty. Its green mountains are the first to catch the rain clouds drifting in from the Atlantic. The slopes that separate the White Towns are often thickly wooded and conceal some botanic rarities: most notably the Spanish fir or *Abies pinsapo,* which only grows in four locations over 1,000 m – all kept under guard and only accessible with a permit.

■■■ **ROUTE ONE: 107 KM**

Grazalema

Don't be surprised if it's raining here: Grazalema is reputed to be the wettest place in Spain. The rainfall, however, tends to be concentrated in the winter; summer can be extremely dry. Otherwise Grazalema's fame rests on its having been the subject of Julian Pitt-Rivers' 1954 classic sociological study *The People of the Sierra*; and on its traditional weaving industry (see below).

Overlooked by towering limestone crags, Grazalema is as good a compendium as any of the vernacular architecture of the White Towns: chalk-coated walls broken up by windows covered with long *rejas* (iron grilles), often reaching to the ground and decorated with flower pots. The Spanish fir tree growing in the main square may be the closest you get to this scarce species. For an overview of the town climb to the viewpoint near the 18thC San José chapel.

Grazalema
(*hotel,*
Grazalema)

As yet the only hotel in town, the Grazalema is a modern place built in sympathy with the local style. There are spectacular views down the valley from its swimming pool and balconies. *Tel 956-13 21 87.*

From the main square of Grazalema take the road down towards Ronda. Before the rose-bedecked petrol station take the steep cobbled track to the left to visit a traditional textile workshop.

Artesania
Textil de
Grazalema

The traditional woollen industry has recently been revived with the aid of government grants. This small factory, open to the public, makes blankets and ponchos from local wool using hand-operated looms and antique machinery. Products are on sale in the adjacent shop. *Closed August.*

Continue down the Ronda road and look out for a right turning marking a short detour to an ancient fountain where eight grotesque heads spout (non-drinking) water from their mouths.

Some 4 km from Grazalema, turn left for Ronda. The road traverses extensive groves of cork oak, their bark surgically skinned once every nine years. Turn right at the T-junction after 12 km and right again shortly on to the C339, again towards Ronda.

After descending a wooded valley you emerge on the farmland around Ronda. Take the left turning to Ronda la Vieja and Setenil ①. This winding lane climbs quickly through pretty countryside and levels out to give views of the Sierra de Grazalema. Some 11 km from the main road fork left on to the MA449 for Ronda la Vieja, less than a kilometre away, and park in the car park.

Ronda la
Vieja

The Roman settlement Acinipo, known locally as Old Ronda, was inhabited from the 1stC BC to the 4thC AD, although there is evidence of human occupation dating back to the Stone Age.

• *Ronda la Vieja, Acinipo.*

Occupying a strategic position above the Vale of Ronda this is an atmospheric spot for a picnic. Behind a tall wall is an amphitheatre cut out of the rock. The hill terminates in the abrupt 999-metre crest of a cliff giving magnificent views of Grazalema and its surrounding mountains. Admission is free, but register with the caretaker at the gate before making the stiff ten-minute uphill walk.

Return to the fork and turn left to take the MA486 following the contours down towards Setenil. Turn right at the crossroads, again for Setenil. There are views to the left over the roof tops of the village as you enter. Parking on this stretch of road is hazardous. Continue until you reach the bottom of the hill and park near the bridge.

Setenil de las Bodegas

Setenil is the most curious and atypically sited of the White Towns. Rather than exploiting a lofty defensive position, it winds through a small gorge, using the rock overhangs as roofs for some of the houses; one street is a tunnel. The 16thC church stands on a rock in the middle of the village next to an Arab tower (under restoration). From its battlements you get an interesting view of the town.

Las Flores
(*restaurant, Setenil*)

A noisy village bar with tables on a splendid balcony overlooking the gorge. The pork, lamb and seafood dishes are simply prepared and served without formality. The restaurant is reached from below by the provocatively named street, Spanish Gibraltar. *Tel 956 13 42 00; price band A.*

From the bridge take the CA422 towards Arriate and turn right on

• Narrow, stepped street, Setenil de las Bodegas.

leaving the town for Arriate and Ronda, immediately crossing a small bridge. After passing through the hamlets of Los Prados and La Cimada you reach Arriate, a well-kept town. Leaving the town the road follows a railway line for a few kilometres. Turn right at the next major junction on to the C341 for Ronda. Follow the signs under the railway bridge, forking right into Ronda to enter the city along the Avenida Málaga. Follow the signs for Centro Ciudad, Puente Nuevo and Plaza de Toros. Park in the car park between the bullring and Bar Jerez, or in one of the streets nearby.

Ronda

The most famous of the White Towns, Ronda is also the most visited, because of its proximity to the Costa del Sol. The town edges up to a tall cliff face and is divided in two by the narrow 90-metre deep gorge of the River Guadalevín. An impressive 18thC bridge, Puente Nuevo, joins the old and new parts of town. Its central section was formerly used as a prison. The bullring, in the new town, is the oldest in Spain and has a renowned museum of bullfighting. The modern form of bullfighting, on foot rather than on horseback, originated here in the 18thC; to commemorate this, a special bullfight in period dress, the Corrida Goyesca, is held in September.

The old Moorish town on the other side of the gorge, which has several Renaissance palaces, needs to be explored at leisure. For the classic, much-photographed view of Puente Nuevo, either take the path down into the gorge from Plaza del Campillo (at the end of Calle Tenorio) or drive down Camino de los Molinos (from the Almocabar Gate) and climb up to the Arabic Arch.

Reina Victoria *(hotel, Ronda)* A large green-roofed building with turn-of-the-century elegance, the Reina Victoria has been refurbished but lacks a few comforts. It trades mainly on its past: you are not allowed to forget that the Austrian poet Rainer Maria Rilke stayed here in 1913. An extensive garden and terrace give stunning views over the surrounding countryside. *Tel 952 87 12 40; price band C.*

Leave the city in the direction of Seville (along Calle Sevilla), turning left on to the C339 for Jerez and Sevilla. After about 2 km turn left off this road for Benaoján and Cortes de la Frontera. For some way the road runs under crags inhabited by vultures. It then enters the Grazalema nature reserve, crosses a little river and the Bobadilla-Algeciras railway, and starts climbing.

Molino del Santo *(hotel, Benaoján)* *Turn left (signposted) and negotiate the little lanes behind the station.* This is a disused watermill converted into a discreet sun-trap by British owners Andy Chapell and Pauline Elkin. There is a back-drop of rushing water. You can eat here too. *Tel 952 16 71 51; price band B.*

Continue into Benaoján and keep straight on (bearing right at the lampost-roundabout) along the avenue with flowers in the middle. Turn left at the T-junction at the end of the town for Cueva de la Pileta. The cave is up a short drive after 4.5 km. A short flight of stone steps takes you from the car park to the entrance.

Cueva de la Pileta This extensive cave contains one of the best collections of neolithic and paelaeolithic art in Europe. The paintings in La Pileta are contemporary with or earlier than the more famous ones at Altamira in northern Spain, but this cave has not been adapted to tourism in any way. Part of the charm of a visit is the way in which tours are conducted. Entrance is limited to groups of 25, carrying pressure lamps (it's advisable to take your own torch).

The cave may have been inhabited 25,000 years ago. Fragments of pots — thought to be the oldest ceramics in Europe — were found here. The walls are adorned with yellow and red symbols and paintings. Black characters, thought to be a kind of occult writing, are yet to be deciphered. The most famous drawing is of a giant fish, more than a metre long. *Tours on the hour from 9-2 and 4-7, lasting about one hour.*

Return towards Benaoján, but don't turn into the village. Carry straight on towards Montejaque, another white town lying in a hollow in the hills. Bear right around the town for Ronda. The road passes through a short stony gorge before dropping down to meet the C339 by the Venta la Vega bar. Turn left. Take the next left turn to Grazalema and turn left again shortly afterwards to return the way you came through the cork woods. Turn right at the T-junction after 12 km for Grazalema.

ROUTE TWO: 110 KM

Take the road out of Grazalema which curves up past El Tajo restaurant and climbs along the slope behind the town. A few kilometres out of town, turn left for El Bosque (17 km) and Arcos (50 km). After negotiating the El Boyar Pass (1,103 metres), where there is a lay-by (great views), you drop down to Benamahoma (off the road).

Linares
(restaurant, Benamahoma)

Fresh trout is the main item on the menu in this restaurant, situated in a pretty valley next to the municipal swimming pool and fish farm. Open daily in Jul, Aug and Sep. The rest of the year only at weekends. *No telephone; price band A. Continue towards El Bosque and turn right at the T-junction into the village.*

El Bosque

Skirting the town centre (to your right), turn off left to the Nature Reserve Information Centre where there is ample car parking. The Centre distributes leaflets on graded walks in the reserve.

Continue on the C344, taking a left turning outside El Bosque for Arcos de la Frontera. After crossing farmland, the strikingly sited town of Arcos appears ahead, hanging over a cliff face above the River Guadalete. *After crossing the dam turn left for Conjunto Monumental and follow these signs all the way to the top of the town, passing along narrow streets and under the buttresses of the church of Santa Maria. Turn right, still up the hill, and park in the uppermost square, Plaza Cabildo, outside the church and the Parador,* a state-run hotel with views from most rooms, *tel 956 70 05 00.*

Arcos de la Frontera

The buildings of the old town creep right up to the lip of the precipice. A balcony on the edge of the Plaza Cabildo provides views over the surrounding countryside. The Church of Santa María de la Asunción

• Plaza Cabildo, Arcos de la Frontera.

has a magnificent though weather-worn Plateresque façade. (Plateresque is a 16thC style of intricately carved stonework.)

El Convento
(*hotel/ restaurant, Arcos*)

A family-run establishment in two buildings 50 metres apart. The restaurant (*tel 956 70 32 22, price band A/B*) is in a former 16thC palace around a tiny patio. The quaint eight-bed hotel occupies part of a convent; *tel 956 70 23 33; price band A/B*.

Leave the square the way you came in and follow the one-way system signposted Salida Ciudad through tight streets, some of them only just wide enough for a car. As you emerge from the old town, look for the signs to El Bosque, bearing right to cross the metal bridge, Puente San Miguel. Turn left at the end of the bridge and fork left for El Bosque. Fork left again by the restaurant (passing the turning to El Algar on your right, which leads to Cortijo Faín – see page 188). When you reach the junction beside the sand works (on your right), turn right for El Bosque. (An alternative, if you get lost in the maze of streets in Arcos, is to leave the town on the N342 for Bornos and Ronda and to turn right off it when the road straightens out for El Bosque and Ubrique, crossing the dam below Arcos).

Cortijo Faín
(hotel, Arcos de la Frontera)

Turn left off the El Algar road after 3 km into the hotel drive. You will find a whitewashed country residence grouped around a spotless courtyard and surrounded by olive groves. The ten large bedrooms are all distinctively-styled, furnished with antiques. *Tel 956 70 11 67; price band C.*

Soon after leaving Arcos the road to El Bosque climbs a hill. When it starts to lose height, turn left ② for Villamartín and Puerto Serrano. Along this road, which crosses the Villamartín agricultural plain, there are views to the left of Bornos, another White Town, which sits beside a reservoir. *Go straight over the crossroads by the solitary farmhouse. Soon the road rounds a tight bend to reach a T-junction. Turn right for Prado del Rey and El Bosque.* You pass the 16thC shrine to Nuestra Señora de las Montañas on the right. On a hill to the left sits the stump of Villamartín castle.

Prado del Rey

Unlike the other White Towns this one was founded quite recently, in the 18thC, in order to bring agricultural labour to the area. Many of its inhabitants live from leather working and, if you ask around, you can buy inexpensive belts, bags, purses and wallets. It has a pretty tree-lined main street.

About 2 km beyond Prado del Rey, turn left for Zahara, re-entering the Grazalema Nature Reserve. This gentle road passes through farmland over the unmarked and undramatic Aguacil Pass. Zahara appears ahead. *At the stop sign at the end of the road turn right up the hill into Zahara and park in or near the main square. There's also a car park on the way out of the town towards Grazalema.*

Zahara de la Sierra

A tightly-knit white village zig-zagging up the foot of a rock crowned by a rebuilt castle keep, Zahara is arguably the prettiest and best kept of the White Towns. The ascent to the superbly restored 10thC Arab castle (built on Roman foundations) takes ten to 15 minutes; views from the battlements. Zahara stages a spectacular Corpus Christi celebration in June when the streets and walls disappear under a mass of greenery.

Marqués de Zahara
(hotel, Zahara)

The light, leafy central patio and delightful bar and dining room of this little hotel in a 17thC building are, sadly, somewhat let down by the careless furnishing of the bedrooms. *Tel 956 12 30 61; price band A. From the main square of Zahara take the road towards Grazalema (beginning as the Calle Ronda). Turn right for Grazalema on to a road cut into the mountainside which snakes up to the Las Palomas Pass (1,357*

• *Zahara de la Sierra, possibly the prettiest of the White Towns.*

metres), stunning views all the way.

Garganta Verde   On the ascent you pass a locked gate on the right leading to Garganta Verde, a dramatic walk beneath a vulture colony. It can only be visited on guided tours when the vultures are not nesting (apply at the nature reserve information centre in Zahara or tel 956 12 31 14). From the next locked gate on the right (giving access to another restricted nature trail, Puerto de Acebuches) you can watch vultures wheeling over the crags of Garganta Verde.

After the exposed heights of the pass the road winds down into pine woods. On the right is the entrance to one of the principal Spanish fir forests (access by permission only).

Some kilometres further on you come out of the woods above the roof tops of Grazalema, descending to the main square by the road on which you began.

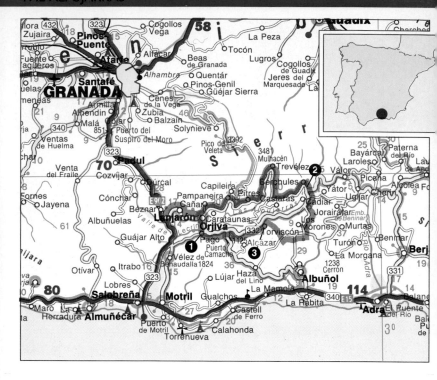

Far below Spain's two highest peaks, Mulhacén and Veleta, the southern slopes of the Sierra Nevada slide into the quaint valleys of the Alpujarras.

Compact white villages cling to steep but fertile mountain sides carved into innumerable terraces. The houses cluster together as if built on top of each other at random; flat roofs, supported on crooked chestnut beams, sprout quaint chimneys of all shapes and sizes. These villages are unmistakably of Arab origin: the Alpujarras were the last refuge of the Moors in Spain when the Kingdom of Granada was conquered in 1492. The only other place you'll see this curious architecture is in the Atlas mountains of Morocco.

In recent years the back-breaking labour of hill-farming has driven most of the young to the cities. Their places have been taken by urban Spaniards and foreigners seeking an alternative rural lifestyle. Despite this influx of outsiders, the Alpujarras remain surprisingly unspoilt. In more remote villages the

• *Ploughing in a vineyard, La Contraviesa.*

inhabitants will stare unashamedly at you as if you had arrived from Mars.

Roads now reach almost everywhere in this region, but the contours favour exploration on foot. Only by taking the little paths that meander along the terraces will you get a glimpse of the real Alpujarras. If you don't have time to walk, the circular driving route given here will at least introduce you to this fascinating area. With curves almost all the way, distances are deceptive and you should allow more time than the map suggests. Not recommended to those who suffer from car sickness.

ROUTE: 137 KM

Lanjarón

Eight springs with differing medicinal properties attract a steady stream of health-seekers to this spa in season; they also supply bottled water to the rest of Spain. Locally made wickerwork is on sale in shops on the main street. The only accommodation that doesn't have the spa institutional smell is the Miramar (*tel 958 77 01 61*). It's comfortable enough despite a clash of decorative styles.

Leave Lanjarón on the road to Orgiva, where you have a choice of one large and two small petrol stations at which to fill up. After crossing the River Lanjarón, look back for views of the town and its ruined castle, stranded on a rock. The castle held out after the fall of Granada in 1492 until Ferdinand of Aragon blasted it to bits in 1500. In despair, its

• *Traditional Alpujarran rugs, Pampaneira.*

defeated commander threw himself over the battlements.

A winding road takes you first across terraces of olive groves and then through scrubland before descending to Orgiva on the lush floor of a valley. *Don't cross the bridge to enter the town. Instead turn left* ① *beside the Alpujarra Grill for Trevélez and Pitres.* The road climbs quickly round the slopes above Orgiva, passing Sortes Cave on the left which was used as a refuge in the Civil War and at Christmas serves as the setting for a 'living crib'. Carataunas, a short distance below the road on the right, has some pretty streets and typical Alpujarran architecture.

Leaving behind the lush vegetation of the lower valley you ascend drier, wilder slopes scattered with a few olive trees. A forest track to the left leads to the Buddhist meditation centre of O Sel Ling. In 1987 the Spanish news media focused on the centre when a small boy named Osel, son of a local bricklayer, was acclaimed by the Tibetan Buddhists as the reincarnation of a lama.

Barranco de Poqueira   After rounding a corner marked by the shrine of Padre Eterno you enter the leafy Barranco de Poqueira (Poqueira Valley), the prettiest part of the Alpujarras, and the most visited. The villages of Pampaneira and Bubión appear ahead as white splashes on the hillside, echoing the permanent snow on the peaks of the Sierra Nevada above. There are shady stopping places along this stretch, and footpaths up and down the steep slopes. At the head of the valley the road crosses the River Poqueira, passes a hydroelectric power station and winds upwards into Pampaneira.

Pampaneira   The sign at the entrance to the village reads: 'Traveller, stop and live here with us'. Most tourists, however, halt at the first of the three villages in the Barranco de Poqueira to shop for souvenirs, especially colourful rugs. Cars are barred from Pampaneira's narrow streets, but

• *Early morning, Bubión church and surrounding fields.*

there is an ample car park on the left as you enter the village. Two modest bar-restaurants have roof-top terraces on the main square. The name of the village is Galician in origin, recording the Alpujarras' change in ownership and fortune. After the Moriscos (Moors who had nominally converted to Christianity after the Reconquest) were expelled in 1609, the area was repopulated with settlers from northern Spain. These inexperienced new arrivals were unable to maintain the prodigious agricultural productivity of the Moriscos and the terraces were gradually given over to subsistence farming.

The road continues upwards. Passing above the village you have a view of the flat grey roofs of the houses and their unusual chimneys. *When the road levels out, turn left for Bubión. Park on the roadside to explore the village on foot; then keep going up the hill towards Capileira.*

Villa Turística de Bubión (hotel, Bubión)   An attractive mini-Alpujarran village of self-contained 'houses', with a choice of restaurant or self-catering kitchenette, and run by obliging staff. Guided walking tours can be arranged. *Tel 958 76 31 11; price band A/B.*

Capileira   If you only have time to walk around one village in the Alpujarras, make sure it's this one. Capileira, with its steep, narrow streets and photogenic corners, is a compendium of the areas' vernacular

• *Distinctive Alpujarran chimney, Capileira.*

architecture, popular with artists. Near the church is a museum housing a collection of rural artefacts and dedicated to the 19thC travel writer, Pedro de Alarcón, who first put the Alpujarras on the map. At the bottom of the village there are some fine examples of *tinao*: a bridge joining two houses, turning the street into a tunnel.

The best places to eat at in Capileira are Mesón Poqueira (*tel 958 763048; price band B*), which has simple bedrooms above; and Casa Ibero, also known as Mesón Alpujareño (*tel 958 763006; closed Sun evening and Mon; price band B*). For tea try the German-run Café Europa, which serves home-made cakes.

The Veleta Road (*detour*) From Capileira the road continues over the Sierra Nevada to Granada, degenerating a few kilometres from the village into a dirt track, only passable in summer, and after checking with the local police. When it reaches the summit of Spain's second highest peak, El Veleta (3,398 metres) it becomes a surfaced road again – the highest in Europe. If you stay in Capileira in winter you can drive up to the snowline and down to the Mediterranean coast in the same day.

Return down the valley via Bubión to the junction beyond it and turn left to continue towards Trevélez along a road which twists around the mountain side giving tremendous views.

If you want to explore some pretty and relatively unvisited corners of the Alpujarras, turn off along this next stretch of the road. Ferreirola and Atalbeitar (on the other side of Pitres), both at the end of lanes down the hill to the right, retain much of their original character in spite of the numbers of foreigners who have bought village houses. From any of the villages on or off the road numerous paths lead between the (often disused) terraces; across deep ravines; through chestnut and poplar woods which turn mellow colours in autumn; past abandoned stone-studded threshing floors and bubbling springs; and over irrigation ditches which seem to appear from nowhere, merrily gurgling with meltwater from the Sierra Nevada. The occasional mulberry tree is a reminder of the Alpujarra's silk industry – silkworms will only eat mulberry leaves – which flourished under Moorish occupation and languished after the expulsion of the Moriscos.

Pitres and Pórtugos
If you want a walk but don't want to stray too far off the road, park in the square of Pitres and take the path up through the woods to the hamlet of Capilerilla. The new camping site and restaurant, before reaching Pitres, (*tel 958 766111; price band A*) has a swimming pool with sensational views. The skyline of neighbouring Pórtugos is broken by a multi-storey hotel, Nuevo Malagueño, which offers guests memorable views from its balconies (*tel 958 766098*).

A short way after Pórtugos you cross a bridge with a chapel on the left. Park in the small car park on the right.

Fuente Agria and El Chorreón
A few steps beside the chapel lead down to the Fuente Agria, a spring from which six tubes spout iron-rich water staining the rocks a rusty red. From the car park/picnic area a longer flight of steps leads down to El Chorreón waterfall hidden in a small ravine dripping with foliage.

After Busquistar you leave behind the mild micro-climate of the western Alpujarras and traverse mixed woodland of oak and pine to emerge on the exposed slopes around Trevélez, which have a distinctly Alpine feel.

Trevélez
At 1,500 metres Trevélez is the highest village in Spain, indeed one of the highest in Europe. The cold climate is ideal for curing hams – which

have an international reputation. Like many settlements in the Alpujarras it is divided into separate parts or *barrios*. The lower *barrio*, on the main road, is the least attractive. To see the most picturesque streets, drive up to the middle part of the village and park in the Plaza del Barrio Medio. Barrio Alto is reached from here by a short lane. In August, a pilgrimage leaves the village on foot, horseback and in vehicles to celebrate mass on the summit of Spain's highest mountain, Mulhacén, 3,482 metres.

Mesón La Fragua
(*hotel/restaur ant, Trevélez*)

The hotel and restaurant are in separate buildings in Barrio Medio. There are views over the roof tops and down the valley from the upstairs dining room which is furnished in polished pine. The renovated hotel building dates from 1770 and some of the rooms have ceilings of exposed slate. Others share a roof-top terrace. *Tel 958 85 85 73; closed two weeks in Feb; price band A/B.*

Leave Trevélez by the road for Bérchules and Cádiar, continuing along some wild slopes. Keep straight on for Juviles; or if you have time to spare, take the alternative route described below.

Castarás and Nieles
(*alternative route*)

This variation of the route, which adds 9 km and is not suitable for wide vehicles, visits two villages well off the beaten track.

Take the right turning to Castarás from a tight bend in the road. Take the next left turning, again signposted Castarás.

Castarás's old church (the keys are kept in a neighbouring house) is affectionately known as 'the cathedral of the Alpujarras'. Its interior was gutted by communists in the Civil War but has since been refurbished. The influence of Morisco craftsmen can be clearly seen in the beams overhead.

The little road to Nieles (unsignposted and not marked on most maps) starts beside the church. The chimney on the hillside to the left is all that remains of long-abandoned mercury mines. There's only just enough room for the average saloon car to squeeze between two walls as the lane passes through the bottom of Nieles. It then climbs steeply over rocky moorland to Juviles. *Turn right to rejoin the route.*

After Juviles you cross an unmarked pass to reach Bérchules. The road descends in curves to a bridge and climbs again to ② *a junction above Cádiar. Take the right turning towards Cádiar and Torvizcón.*

Yegen (*22-km detour*)

Turn left at the junction ②, in the direction of Ugíjar. The only reason to seek out the small village of Yegen is to see the home (marked by a plaque) of the British writer and Hispanicist Gerald Brenan who came here in 1920 in search of peace and cheap living. Then the Alpujarras were only accessible on foot or muleback. That didn't discourage Lytton Strachey and Virginia Woolf from visiting him – although the former complained that riding on a mule exacerbated his piles. Brenan himself thought nothing of walking here from Granada over the Sierra

Nevada. *South from Granada* (published in 1957), his account of local life, traditions, flora, ancient history, as well as his own experiences, is required reading for anyone interested in the Alpujarras.

Cádiar

A sizeable settlement on the flat valley floor overshadowed by sparse hills, Cádiar has not much to offer the tourist except a petrol station – even though the sign at the entrance boasts several attractions. If you are here during the local fiesta in early October, free wine is served from a bar.

Bear left at the petrol station at the entrance to Cádiar for Albuñol and Albondón. As you climb into the Sierra de la Contraviesa, there are views of the Alpujarras behind. Take the right turning on to the GR443 for Haza de Lino and Orgiva. This road runs for miles along the seaward side of the mountain range, just below the summit. You can see the coast in places. The locals claim you can also see the mountains of Africa on a clear day.

Sierra de la Contraviesa

Running parallel to the Sierra Nevada but half as high, the rounded tops of the Contraviesa are stippled with almond trees and vines. These vineyards, at 1,300 metres, are supposedly the highest in Europe, enjoying a benign microclimate. A native grape variety is used to produce a light rosé wine. Farming these slopes is labour-intensive – animals have to be used in place of machinery – and as a consequence the wine industry is gradually shrinking.

Take the right turning to Torvizcón, descending a steep and often unprotected lane down a ridge. At the T-junction in the valley ③ turn left.

Torvizcón

The *bodega* at the end of Calle Aguilera will draw Contraviesa wine for you from 200-year-old oak barrels. This unbottled wine, sometimes known as Costa, is normally drunk young and doesn't travel. The recently-created bottled varieties of Contraviesa wine are a poor substitute for the real thing.

From Torvizcón an improved road follows the narrowing valley to come out above Orgiva. At the next junction turn right. As you descend there are views across the wide valley towards Capileira and Bubión in the distance. You are heading into a tunnel; but turn right at its mouth and cross the bridge into Orgiva.

Orgiva

The shopping and administrative centre of the western Alpujarras, Orgiva lacks attractions of its own. The closest contender is its twin-towered yellowish Baroque church. Many of the stallholders in the Thursday market are foreigners who live in the surrounding villages. *Carry on through the town towards Lanjarón, crossing the bridge over a dry river bed and reaching the junction in front of Alpujarra Grill. Keep straight on for Lanjarón.*

• *Cabo de Gata.* You may have seen the lunar landscapes of Almería already. Europe's only true desert – shielded from wet Atlantic winds by a chain of high mountains – has been used as a backdrop for countless films, from *Lawrence of Arabia* to Spaghetti westerns.

Spain's south-eastern corner may be hot, dry and sparsely vegetated, but Almería is more than a gigantic film set and it conceals many picturesque and interesting spots. Occasional clumps of date palm lounging above cubic white houses lend a North African air. Parts of the lowlands have been transformed by an agricultural revolution, with vast tracts of otherwise infertile land swathed in moisture-retaining plastic to grow early vegetable crops.

This circuit, around the perimeter of the Sierra Alhamilla, crosses the inland desert and reaches a climax in the volcanic headland of Cabo de Gata, the driest part of Europe and a nature reserve which boasts some of the few remaining unspoilt beaches on Spain's Mediterranean coast.

Roads are sparse, and this route is only possible making use of some (uncongested) main roads. The several detours – one of

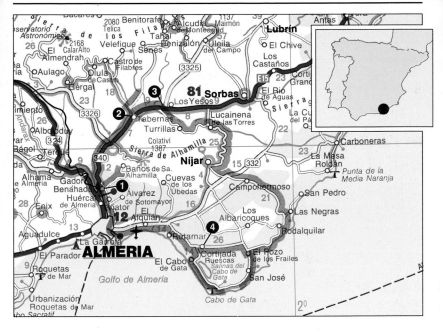

them using an unsurfaced but easily passable track – link the route to some of the province's best sights.

If possible, don't visit the area during the fierce summer. The winters, in contrast, are warm and agreeable, with the advantage of fewer visitors. Off the main roads and out of season, this is where you'll find Spain's truly undiscovered backroads.

■ ROUTE: 180 KM

Almería

Founded as a port by the Phoenicians, Almería was an important city (and sometime pirate base) under the Moors who named it `Mirror of the Sea'. Nowadays it is a small provincial capital exporting grapes and minerals. It is one of the only two cities in Spain where bars serve free tapas with drinks (the other is Granada) – try especially those in the streets around Calle Trajano.

The most conspicuous monument is the Alcazaba, a sprawling, ruined Arab hill-top fortress built in the 10th and 11thC, with gardens inside and views over the city from its walls. Behind the Alcazaba is the Centre for the Rescue of Saharan Fauna (visited by prior arrangement only), a scientific research station exploiting Almería's arid climate in the cause of endangered desert species. The city's 16thC cathedral, fortified against Barbary pirates, has a fine Renaissance portal.

Torreluz IV
(*hotel,*
Almería)

With its white leather armchairs, spiral staircase and roof-top swimming-pool this is the smartest accommodation in the centre of the city. If you are on a tight budget, across the square are a three-star and two-star hotel (Torreluzs III and II) run by the same management. *Tel 950 23 47 99; price band C.*

Bellavista
(*restaurant,*
Almería)

To get to Almería's most acclaimed restaurant, lost in drab surroundings several kilometres from the city centre, take the motorway towards the airport and turn off at the Viator exit. The restaurant is signposted from there. The menu, strong on fish and seafood, varies daily according to the market. Bellavista claims to have one of the most comprehensive restaurant wine cellars in Spain. *Tel 950 29 71 56; closed Sun and Mon evening; price band C.*

Leave Almería through unpromising scenery on the N340 north in the direction of Murcia and Granada.

Balneario de
Sierra
Alhamilla
(*hotel,*
Pechina)

To reach the hotel, leave the N340 for Chuche and turn right after the town for Pechina. Just before Pechina, turn left for the Balneario de Sierra Alhamilla; turn right shortly after for Sierra Alhamilla. Although set in the desolately dry foothills of the Sierra Alhamilla, this spa, restored to its original 18thC glory by its owner, Isidro Pérez, is an oasis of beauty. (It makes a pleasant alternative starting point for the route, too.) Beneath the hotel are Roman baths, also modern spa facilities. Two minutes' walk away is a swimming pool filled with natural hot water, which makes for a relaxing plunge after a day's driving.

Los Millares
(*24-km*
detour)

For this detour, to the prehistoric site of Los Millares, ① turn left off the N340 in Benahadux for Gador and Las Alpujarras. Some cave houses line the road. Some 7 km after Gador you reach Los Millares on the right: a fenced enclosure behind what looks like an abandoned building but which is really the guard post. Leave your passport with the guard and drive or walk down the track.

Considered to be one of Europe's most important Bronze-Age sites, Los Millares was occupied between 2700 and 1800 BC when it was next to a navigable river as well as the all-important copper mines. The four defensive walls and necropolis have been partially rebuilt. You can crawl inside one of the igloo-shaped tombs through three circular openings. The bright blue birds which are a common sight around here are rollers. *Open Tues to Sat 9.30 am-2 pm and 4-6 pm (winter) or 9.30 am-1.30 pm and 7-9.30 pm (summer); Sun 9.30 am-2.30 pm; closed Mon.*

Return to the N340 by the way you came.

• *Yucca City, scene of many a western shoot-out.*

From Benahadux carry on north crossing a viaduct over the River Andarax to enter the desert of Tabernas: a parched land of pointed grey hills, badlands and canyons. Turn right for Tabernas and Murcia, still on the N340.

Mini-Hollywood

Also known as Yucca City, and built by Sergio Leone to shoot early Clint Eastwood classics such as *A Fistful of Dollars*, this is the most extensive and well organized of the three film sets in the Almerian Desert which are now run as mini-theme parks. Before the boom ended, a hundred westerns had been made in this mock cowboy town, with the locals playing Mexicans and Indians. It is still used occasionally for shooting TV commercials. Unless you want to watch a mock gunfight in the streets, a hanging, a bank robbery, a stage coach hold-up or a brawl in the saloon, you can get the flavour of Yucca City from the car park across the ravine without paying the entrance fee. *Open 9 am-6 pm (winter) and 9 am-9 pm (summer).*
Continue to Tabernas, overlooked by the remains of its Moorish castle.

Solar Energy Plant
(*detour*)

After by-passing Tabernas turn off ② for Tahal, crossing the main road and carrying straight on for Plataforma Solar – about 10 km.
The plant is run as an international experiment in harnassing Almería's abundant sunshine to feed power into the national grid. Banks of reflectors concentrate the sun's rays on to a shining receiver

• *Turillas.*

dish at the top of a white tower. Beside the gate there's space to park and look through the fence. You can visit the centre, by prior arrangement (*tel 950 36 51 89*), on Wednesday and Thursday mornings.

Return to the main road the way you came.

About 5 km beyond Tabernas turn right ③ after a discothèque to the lane for Turillas which crosses a plain and climbs to a junction on the hillside. Turn right for Turillas.

Turillas

This small village of pretty white houses has only one asset: its panoramic view sweeping west to east from the Tabernas Desert almost to the coast, and north across the plain to the Sierra de Filabres. As good a vantage point as any is the yellow and white domed shrine of Saint Anthony which you reach just before the town.

From Turillas return to the last junction and turn right for Lucainena de las Torres. The road winds around the hillside giving, to begin with, the same fine views to the left.

At the junction beside Lucainena turn right for Níjar. For the next 20 km you are on a lonely road which winds around the eastern flank of the Sierra Alhamilla, a dry landscape dotted with spiky bushes. The few houses you pass are low, white cubic structures. Coming down from the Sierra you have views of the vast plastic greenhouses that surround Campohermoso.

Níjar

The principal town in this corner of the province, Níjar was a poor place until the coming of plastic greenhouse farming. Until then it made a living from hand-made rugs (*jarapas*) and multi-coloured glazed pottery. These can both be bought as souvenirs. Most of the potters' workshops (some of which can be visited) are on Real de las Eras Street. Authentic Níjar pots are green, brown, blue and yellow. The blue and white ones are made for tourists.

Signposting through Níjar is inadequate. Two roads descend to the plain below: take the more northerly one, not the one signposted for Almería. You should come to a junction with grain silos beside it. Turn left through a small gorge and over a bridge. Cross the N344 dual carriageway for Campohermoso. (If you do take the wrong road out of Níjar, you will come to a left turning to Carboneras. Take this and it will bring you to the junction by the grain silos. Keep straight on to rejoin the route).

Keep straight on through Vistabella and Campohermoso, one of the towns which has most benefited from Almería's agricultural revolution. Carry on for Las Negras, cutting through threadbare hills and by-passing Fernán Pérez (where you enter the Cabo de Gata Nature Reserve) and Las Hortichuelas.

Fork left for a detour to visit Las Negras (2.5 km), a small resort on a shingle beach, or turn right to continue the route to Rodalquilar, a short way off the road.

Rodalquilar The spookily abandoned workings of the Iberian peninsula's only gold mines are about half a kilometre above the town along a bumpy track, just passable by car. Crumbling staircases used only by lizards (ascend at your own peril) lead to skeletal buildings towering above the gigantic concrete pans used to sieve the ore. The Phoenicians dug the first mines here. The latest attempt to reactivate them came to an end in the 1960s.

Carry on along the main road from Rodalquilar to meet the coast at Mirador de la Amatista, a cliff-top car-park and balcony. The next settlement you reach is La Isleta (again off the road), an impoverished fishing village of flat-topped white houses at the base of a small peninsula with a stony beach to either side.

At the T-junction turn left towards San José. Pozo de los Frailes preserves the ill-cared-for remains of a horizontal waterwheel which was once driven by a donkey.

San José The only holiday resort of any size on this stretch of coast, San José has been described as a town in which the building never stops. Fortunately, most of the houses and apartments are low-rise and vaguely conform to the local cubic style of architecture. The season is short for San José and for much of the year there are few people on

• *San José.*

the streets. The newsagent who runs the kiosk on the main street is an excellent source of information about the Cabo de Gata Nature Reserve (see opposite).

San José
*(hotel/
restaurant,
San José)*

With an ingenuous colour scheme and eccentric furnishings, the San José has far more character than any other hotel around here. Fans whirr overhead; a parrot in a cage in the sitting room is kept covered up to stop it talking. Large windows provide views over the beach and out to sea. *Tel 950 38 0116; closed Jan 15-Mar 15; price band B.*

**Los
Genoveses
and Monsul**
*(10-km
detour)*

Two of the most picturesque and unspoilt beaches in Spain are reached by a passable dirt road from San José. *Carry on past the Hotel San José and take the upper fork, the Camino de Monsul. Signs for Playa de los Genoveses and Playa de Monsul mark the way to a no-through road which becomes a broad and bumpy track passing below a windmill and descending to rich farmland. After 2 km the road forks. Turn left for Los Genoveses, a curving arc of sand between two prominent headlands. Return to the fork and continue on the track to the cove of Monsul.* The distinctive rock in the middle of the sand appeared in a scene in the film *Indiana Jones and the Last Crusade.* From here you can see the old watchtower of Vela Blanca high above the coast. This is the destination of the next detour. The road between these two points is only passable on foot or on horseback.

Botanists are attracted to Cabo de Gata Nature Reserve by the rare flora. It is an area of wild volcanic mountains around the cape with an average annual temperature of over 18 degrees and rainfall of just 200 ml: a natural habitat for drought-resistant plants – including Europe's only native palm – which have their closest relatives in North Africa. A few of these species grow nowhere else in the world. Many of the hillsides are covered with a common, but nonetheless important, plant: esparto grass. Until recently it was harvested to supply a cottage industry making ropes, twines, saddles, baskets and mats.

Return the way you came to San José and leave on the road by which you arrived. Passing through Pozo de los Frailes, keep straight on at the next junction for Almería. After passing the tyre-testing plant ④ turn left for Cabo de Gata. Although this next part of the route is effectively a detour, it's worth the effort for some spectacular scenery.

Cabo de Gata
(20-km detour)

Don't stop in the depressed and sand-swept village of Cabo de Gata, unless you want to eat fresh fish in one of its simple restaurants on the beach. Continue on the long flat road which follows the sea-front towards the mountains around the cape. The salt pans on the left attract great flocks of flamingoes (sometimes numbering more than 2,000), especially in the late summer and early autumn. There's a hide by the water.

After passing the salt works, in which conveyor belts pile the crystals into snow-white conical mountains, the plain ends abruptly. The road becomes steep, narrow and windy as it rises and falls around the coast to reach the cape and lighthouse. A viewpoint hangs over the cliffs. Beneath it the waves break over the jagged rocks of El Arrecife de las Sirenas – Mermaids' Reef. The name refers not to the mythical creature but to a fishermen's nickname for the rare monk seal which inhabited these waters until 1974.

You can turn back here or continue on the surfaced road which twists up steep slopes for the next 3 km (without crash barriers) to the tower of Vela Blanca, standing on the highest headland above the sea. There are great views from this windy, isolated spot but it is not a place to linger in. A fence blocks the way on to the track which leads down and around the cliffs to Monsul.

Return on the same road through Cabo de Gata and turn left for Almería. After the new bridge there is a left turning to an inconspicuous nature reserve information centre. Around it are abandoned sisal fields which were planted in the 1950s and 1960s. They quickly fell into disuse when the introduction of artificial fibres made sisal uneconomical.

Go straight over the roundabout (signposted Almería por la Costa) and follow this road between the coast and the airport runway. At the end of the airport turn left, still for Almería por la Costa, along an unbuilt-up strip of coast to enter Almería on its eastern sea-front.

INDEX